Whatever you thought you knew about Black College Football, Carlos Lock will add to your understanding and appreciation of the game. He paints a vivid picture and transports you through time with his words. He is an HBCU griot. This book should be mandatory reading for all incoming HBCU freshmen to instill pride, provide history lessons, and raise awareness of their rich heritage.

– K. Rich
Long-time Ensley, Alabama,
Community Delegate/Representative

I want to restore HBCU football.

– Deion Sanders
Pro Football Hall of Famer
Head Football Coach, Jackson State University

If you know little or nothing about Black College Football, this book will be an eye-opener. If you're fan already, you'll love the author's passion, commitment, and dedication to the sport and to the important role it plays in African-American culture.

– Ed Linehan
President, Sarasota Jazz Club

As a former Southern University Jaguar football player, I vividly recall the rivalry against Jackson State. Having grown up in Jackson, when I returned to play the home team there, the experience was surreal. In Black College Football, *Carlos Lock captures that time and atmosphere to a tee and argues persuasively for why we should continue to support the game today.*

– Carlos Leach, Esq.
Managing Partner
The Leach Firm, PA

Bardolf & Company

BLACK COLLEGE FOOTBALL
  The Game That Time Forgot

ISBN 978-1-7356502-0-3

Published by Bardolf & Company
www.bardolfandcompany.com

Cover design by *shawcreativegroup.com*

Author photo by Athena Lock

To past, present and future
HBCU alums
and
BCF fans and supporters.

BLACK COLLEGE FOOTBALL

The Game That Time Forgot

Carlos A. Lock

Bardolf & Company
Sarasota, Florida

CONTENTS

Black Football Conferences   7

FOREWORD   11

Chapter 1 – GENESIS   15

Chapter 2 – BOOSTER SUPPORT   21

Chapter 3 – GRAMBLING   29

Chapter 4 – HAMPTON   39

Chapter 5 – THE GOLDEN ERA OF
         STEVE "AIR II" MCNAIR   47

Chapter 6 – HBCU CLASSICS   55

Chapter 7 – FINANCES   65

Chapter 8 – IT HAPPENED ONLY ONCE   73

Chapter 9 – WHAT IS TO BE DONE?   77

CONCLUSION   91

Acknowledgments   97

Appendix – HBCUs   100

Index   104

BLACK FOOTBALL CONFERENCES

There are four African American football conferences in the United States:

Central Intercollegiate Athletic Association (CIAA)
Southern Intercollegiate Athletic Conference (SIAC)
Southwestern Athletic Conference (SWAC)
Mid-Eastern Athletic Conference (MEAC).

The earliest is the Central Intercollegiate Athletic Association (CIAA). Established in 1912, it was initially the Colored Intercollegiate Athletic Association and is the oldest African American Conference. An NCAA Division II conference, it is headquartered in Charlotte, North Carolina and consists of:

Bowie State University
Chowan University
Claflin University (no football team)
Elizabeth City State University
Fayetteville State University
Livingstone College
Johnson C. Smith University
Lincoln University (PA)
Shaw University
St. Augustine's University
Virginia State University
Virginia Union University
Winston-Salem State University

Next came the Southern Intercollegiate Athletic Conference (SIAC). Also, an NCAA Division II conference, it was established in 1913. Headquartered in Atlanta, it consists of:

Albany State University
Benedict College
Central State University
Clark Atlanta University
Fort Valley State University
Kentucky State University
Lane College
LeMoyne-Owen College (no football team)
Miles College
Morehouse College
Paine College (no football team)
Savannah State University
Spring Hill College (no football team)
Tuskegee University

The Southwestern Athletic Conference (SWAC) was established in 1920. Headquartered in Birmingham, Alabama, it is an NCAA FCS (Football Championship Subdivision) and consists of:

Alabama A&M University
Alabama State University
Alcorn State University
Grambling State University
Jackson State University
Mississippi Valley State University
Prairie View A&M University
Southern University
Texas Southern University
University of Arkansas at Pine Bluff

The Mid-Eastern Athletic Conference (MEAC) was established most recently, in 1969. Headquartered in Norfolk, Virginia, it is also NCAA FCS. Its members are:

Bethune-Cookman University
Coppin State University (no football team)
Delaware State University
Florida A&M University
Howard University
University of Maryland Eastern Shore (no football team)
Morgan State University
Norfolk State University
North Carolina A&T State University
North Carolina Central University
South Carolina State University

This was the makeup of the predominantly Black conferences in the NCAA in the spring of 2020 when I started to write this book. Since then, Florida A&M and Bethune Cookman University were approved to move to the Southwestern Athletic Conference (SWAC). There has also been discussion that North Carolina A&T is leaving the Mid-Eastern Athletic Conference (MEAC) to join the Big South Conference. But at the time of publication, however, none of the schools had officially left yet.

FOREWORD

In 2020 in Columbus, Georgia, while I was cooling down after a neighborhood run, a call came through my Power Beats 3 headphones. It was K. Rich, one of my Army buddies. In 2003, we were stationed together in Korea. K. Rich lives in Birmingham, Alabama. He and I go way back. Most importantly, he serves as my concierge for the Magic City Classic football game hosted by Birmingham that pits Alabama State University against Alabama A&M.

K. Rich enhances my experience every year because he knows what events to attend and the best places to eat. He also keeps me out of trouble at the Magic City Classic.

He had me on speakerphone to ask which Black College Football Classic was the best while having a debate with a friend from Florida. The Florida gentleman felt that the Florida Classic was the best classic. This game features Bethune-Cookman University and Florida A&M and is played in Orlando, Florida.

By chance, I had attended the 2016 Florida Classic. My sister-in-law bought me tickets for my birthday that year. The family was enjoying Thanksgiving break in Orlando. I did not tailgate. I did not go to any after parties. I barely watched the game. What I remember was that a Hampton University classmate of mine attended, wearing a HU Pirate shirt.

After I thought about K. Rich's question, I endorsed the Bayou Classic as a better Black College Football's classic. Although I have never attended it, there are good reasons to merit that distinction. The game features Grambling State University Tigers versus Southern University Jaguars. In its heyday, celebrated football coach Eddie Robinson patrolled the sidelines for Grambling, and both teams had athletes that would be drafted to the National Football League. Many would go on to have stellar careers, like Aeneas Williams and Jake Reed. The game is played in the New Orleans Superdome and used to be broadcast live on the NBC television network. Two Black College Football teams on live TV with no tape delay! There were several corporate sponsors, too. Since then, the game has moved to NBC Sports Network. Now, you must have cable or streaming capabilities to watch it, but it is still a first-rate event.

Most importantly, the game takes place in New Orleans where any and everything goes down—good food, good drink, good music! No other BCF classic could match that venue, or any other features for that matter. However, since Hurricane Katrina hit the city in August 2005, the Bayou Classic has not been the same. When most black folks relocated to other states, the game seemed to lose its appeal. Of course, Grambling and Southern alums may feel differently; I welcome the challenge to debate the matter.

At this time, I believe the Magic City Classic in Birmingham, Alabama, holds the distinction as the premier Black College Football classic. This is how I presented it to K. Rich and his Florida friend on the phone. The city starts shutting down on Wednesday to prepare for the number of folks coming to town. The game has a grand marshal (one year, it was actor Don Cheadle). City-run charter buses take spectators to Legion Field to limit traffic. The stadium is always packed to the hilt. Outside, it is a sea of Black folks, with music, food and fraternities—truly a sight to behold. In addition, Birmingham has developed its downtown to recognize Black history, via the Civil Rights Trail. You can visit the 16th Street Baptist Church, which was bombed by white supremacists in 1963, killing four young black girls, or the Negro Southern League Museum for a history of African American baseball. The Negro Southern League served as a minor league for the Negro National and American leagues from 1920 until 1936, when organized baseball was segregated.

K. Rich's Florida friend kept arguing for the Florida Classic, but his only real claim to fame was the after-parties. Of course, he was in his 20s, while I am 40 plus and don't party like I used to. Thus, a classic does not impress me just because it has the most or the best parties. As I said to him: Get some more features before you challenge for the title. BCF classics are much more than a bunch of after-parties.

That night, I could not sleep. All I could think about was the conversation I'd had. Then, it hit me: people truly don't have an appreciation for Black College Football. Suddenly, all the aspects came together of what BCF means to me and the memories that I wanted to share. It was time for me to write this book.

I decided that I wanted it to be a hip pocket guide to Black College Football classics and provide an eyewitness account of forgotten games. I also wanted to highlight why Grambling football is the cornerstone of Black College Football and offer solutions to enhance its experience. Above all, I wanted to preserve the legacy of BCF, not only for alums and future students of historically black colleges and universities (HBCUs), but more importantly, for all African Americans as an essential part of our heritage.

I am a huge fan of folklore. As a Mississippian, Robert Johnson's story intrigues me the most. He is considered the Father of the Blues. As the legend goes, he met the devil at a crossroads and sold his soul to become a great guitar player. He got his wish but, in return, died when he was still young.

I have no desire to meet and bargain with the devil, but I had a dream that I dug Robert Johnson out of his grave. We sat on a couple of head stones and shared a jar of lightning. When the jar was empty, I interred Mr. Johnson in his grave. He whispered, "Son, if you can make it in Mississippi, you can make it anywhere." True story and I ain't lying, but it was a moment I needed to push through what was holding me back. When I doubted my ability to write along the way, I let whispers turn into shouts. I can only hope that the book resounds loudly enough to make a difference for Black College Football in many years to come.

Carlos A. Lock
Columbus, Georgia
November 2020

Chapter 1

GENESIS

Jackson Fair, Jackson Dear.
Thee I Love, My dear ole college home.
Thee I Love, Wherever I may roam.
Jackson Fair, Jackson Dear.

— Jackson State University's
Alma Mater song

I was born November 17, 1976, a little more than a week before Thanksgiving. The holiday was November 25 that year and just in time for my first Thanksgiving football game. I will not pretend that I have any recollections of watching it, or any other football game, before I was eight years old. Jackson State University versus Mississippi Valley State University in October 1984 was the first game I remember. As I got older, the two things that I loved most were sweet potato pie and football.

Growing up in the great state of Mississippi, in the city of Jackson, was not like living in New York, California, or any other state with a professional football team. My "professional" football team was the Jackson State University Tigers aka The Blue Bengals, and it was my first love affair, long before I had my first girlfriend. I attended North Jackson Elementary, and our mascot was a Tiger as well.

I started playing organized football in 4th grade. My first position was defensive back until the coach realized I was the fastest player on the team. He switched me to quarterback and running back during 5th and 6th grade. I don't know what my future would have been if cell phones and American Athletic Union (AAU) football teams had been around during my early years. I would have been more committed to improving my abilities. One of my last games for North Jackson was probably one of my best.

Legendary Coach Leon Campbell was at the game that afternoon. He was the head coach at Powell Junior High School where he led the Trojans to numerous city championships. He was not there to scout me but to support his son. As a running back I always made other players miss by faking them out. Often, that would lead to a long run or to a touchdown. And that is what happened in that game. I scored the touchdown that sealed the victory for my team.

As I approached the sideline, I passed Coach Campbell. When he asked me where I was going to school next year, I replied Powell. I was looking forward to being a Powell Junior High School Trojan. He seemed pleased.

But Coach Campbell was such a hot commodity that he was offered the head coaching job at Murrah High School, and he was gone before I even set foot on the Powell campus. I was sorely disappointed.

In those days, the Jackson Public School system sent students to junior high/middle school from 7th to 9th grade. During the start of my 7th-grade year (1989-1990), Jackson had some of the hottest days in its history. Powell Junior High School did not have air conditioning, so there was early release during the first month of school. I went straight home and never stuck around for football practice, which led to me being kicked off the team and my locker cleared of my football gear.

In 8th grade, I became more resolute and stayed the course, but I was only about 5'7". Early in the year, I banged up my knee badly, which took me off the field to rehab. I had to remind coach that I was hurt because my equipment was removed from my locker again.

Because of my size and other talented players ahead of me, the only time I played was with the 7th-grade team. One of the coaches felt I resembled Lem Barney, who starred at Jackson State in the mid-1960s. Later, he played as a cornerback, return specialist and punter for the Detroit Lions and was elected to the professional football Hall of Fame in 1992. At the time, I had no clue who Lem Barney was and didn't try to educate myself about him either.

As the year was winding down, I figured that 9th grade was going to be my time to showcase my abilities, but it didn't happen. The Jackson Public School System shifted its schooling requirements so that, instead of attending Powell Junior High as a 9th grader, I would be attending Callaway High School. I am sure there were some early signs and meetings behind the scenes, but the news hit me without warning, like an unexpected bolt of lightning. I was crushed.

My neighborhood was only a couple of miles from the school. My brother Robert was a 1990 Callaway graduate, and many of his friends were on the football team. Back then, I took a football everywhere with me. One of the young girls in the neighborhood was dating the starting quarterback for Callaway at that time. I used to play catch with him when he passed our house on the way home from visiting her. When there was no throwing partner, I threw the ball to myself—tossing it in the air, running after it and catching it in mid-flight.

My freshmen year at Callaway was a disaster, to say the least. The school did not have the infrastructure to handle the influx of so many new students, so all of my classes met in a network of portable classrooms, aka trailers. I did not have a locker and had to carry my books with me everywhere. However, I still played football—on the junior varsity team—but my love for the game was slowly fading.

One day, the head football coach approached us 9th graders and said, "If you ain't lifting weights and preparing to play next year, you cannot be in the field house during 7th period." I had never thought much about weight training before. Football came naturally to me. I could run, catch and throw easily. Today, I can still spin it with the best of them. There was a notice for baseball tryouts. I had not played baseball since I was 12, but I went and, low and behold, made the team. Guess who got to hang at the field house in 7th period? Yours truly, as a member of the baseball team.

By then, I lost my desire to play football for good. It is not something that I regret, but God grants certain gifts only for a limited time. I'll be the first to admit that I wasted my athletic talents, although I had an excuse. I could run, catch and had good vision, but I was always short. Despite my abilities, I was always overlooked in favor of players with a taller, bulkier physique.

However, when I entered 10th grade, I grew about six inches. Recognizing the change, the assistant football coaches suggested that I come back out for the team. Had I listened to them and applied myself, I probably would have starred at Callaway and realized my dream to become a Jackson State football player. But I was no longer interested in playing for the high school.

Even though I did not play, I remained close to the game throughout my years at Callaway. I knew all the football players because some of us played ball together in elementary or junior high school. Sometimes, I would go to a Thursday night game to scout a team we were scheduled to play the following week. Even though I was not suiting up, I would always provide my analysis and show up to every home game when I did not have to work at McDonald's. My overcritical dissections of their play would piss some guys off. When a classmate dropped a pass, missed a tackle or failed to make a block, he would get an earful from me on Monday at lunch.

I present this upfront because some people may not like my stance on Black College Football, and that's okay. But just because I did not play on that turf does not mean that I didn't have the ability to do so or an understanding of the game. Although I lost my love and desire in high school to be a Jackson State Tiger football player, the Tigers remained my love. Blue Bengal football was always an integral part of my life. I am what many refer to as a sidewalk alum, someone who supports a school but never attended any classes there. To this day, I look forward to going to the games.

But so much has changed since my early days as a BCF fan.

I watched Jerry Rice, Lewis Tillman, Darion Connor, Shannon Boyd, Steve McNair, and countless other players in Mississippi Veterans Memorial Stadium. I wish I had seen the great Walter Payton—I was too young when he starred at Jackson State—but I watched him on TV when he played in the NFL for the Chicago Bears. Now, it seems, there are no more marquee players in Black College Football. Early on in the National Football League, most Black players came from HBCUs, but those days are gone. Some people suggest that when the University of Alabama played the University of Southern California on September 12, 1970, that was the day "HBCUs lost the corner on the nation's best Black football talent."[1] USC defeated an all-white Alabama team 42-21, boasting an all-Black backfield.

Because of COVID-19, the 2020 NFL draft was conducted virtual. As usual, the Southeastern Conference players dominated the early rounds, but I did not notice a single player drafted from an HBCU at the conclusion of the seven rounds. That surprised me and seemed odd. I posted on Facebook about it, but no one seemed to care or care enough to comment. When I reviewed the ESPN draft tracker, I discovered that there was one HBCU draftee after all—Lachavious Simmons of Tennessee State. He was drafted number 227 in the seventh round by the Chicago Bears.

COVID-19's presence has significantly impacted Black College Football. Morehouse College, an HBCU and SIAC conference member, was one of the first colleges in the nation to suspend its football season. No one praised the college leadership's noble act to protect its athletes. Subsequently, the Central Intercollegiate Athletic Association, Southern Intercollegiate Athletic Conference, Southwestern Athletic Conference and the Mid-Eastern Athletic Conference opted out of the 2020 football season as well. This will impact the opportunities for the players in these conferences to reach the NFL. Most notably, it's an additional impediment to showcase why Black College Football matters.

The Southwestern Athletic Conference plans to play football in the spring. On March 20, 2021, Jackson State is scheduled to play Alabama State in Montgomery. I plan to attend this game to support my Blue Bengals.

---

[1] Jemele Hill in *The Atlantic*, "It's Time for Black Athletes to Leave White Colleges."

Chapter 2

BOOSTER SUPPORT

*I shall pass through this world but once. Any good,
therefore, that I can do or any kindness that I can show
to any human being, let me do it now. Let me not defer
or neglect it. For, I shall not pass this way again.*

—Etienne de Grellet,
French-American Quaker missionary

My neighborhood was located on the North side of Jackson,
Mississippi. There were two Norwood subdivisions, and I lived in
the one directly off Beasley Road. It was a middle-class neighborhood with teachers, car salesmen, insurance providers, and health-
care professionals. Integration in the early 1970s led to white
flight, and by the time I grew up there, I believe only one white
resident remained. One of my neighbors, Mr. Richardson, was a
Black World War II veteran. He was like a grandfather to me. He
taught me how to tie a tie and how to put my fishing rod together.
When I landed in the Army, I often kicked myself for not picking
his brain more than I did when I had the opportunity. I could
have benefited from his experiences.

My neighbor on the other side was Mr. Martin. He had a key
leadership role in the Blue Bengal Athletic Association, Jackson
State's booster club. He would recruit the neighborhood kids to

sell programs at Jackson State home games. From 1990-1992, I didn't miss a single one. That added up to five or so home games per year.

Mr. Martin would give us a heads-up in the middle of the week to let us know what time on Saturday to meet at his house. We would get the word out to the other kids in the neighborhood to see who was interested in volunteering. Back in those days, kickoff was usually around 7:30 p.m., so we met at his house around 5:00. Mr. Martin had a Chevy Blazer, so about ten of us would pile into the truck bound for Mississippi Veterans Memorial Stadium, five miles away. If there was not much traffic, it would only take us 15 minutes to get there.

Because we had programs to unload, we were able to drive inside the stadium. Selling the programs got us into the game for free. We only had to sell them until halftime. After we reconciled our money and the programs we had left, we watched the games like regular fans.

I always wanted a Jackson State victory on the field, but I loved watching the marching band, the Sonic Boom of the South, perform, too. It had a women's dance line, The Prancing J-Settes, that were always soft on the eyes and full of rhythm. At some point during the halftime show, they would move to the front and take the spotlight with a song specifically arranged for them. They also performed certain routines in the stands. When the band played versions of the latest hits on the radio, they were off to the sides. One of my cousins was a member of the Prancing J-Settes from 1995 to 1998, and she told me that they spent a lot of hours practicing alone and with the band. The dance line had a limited number of positions, and they had to compete to maintain their spot for each game!

The team's tiger mascot, Wavee Dave, was fun to watch, too, because he was always up to some hilarious antics. He could be a graceful dancer when the band played, but his sprint from the 50-yard line culminating with a dive into one of the goal posts always got the crowd going.

When it came to selling the programs, this is how the economics worked. Spectators paid $2.00, and we received .25 cents for every program sold. We had to sell 100 just to earn $25. Veterans Stadium had a 70,000-seat capacity, so imagine all the walking we had to do up and down the tiers and through the stands. Plus, this was Jackson, Mississippi in the early 90s, and some of my fellow vendors cut corners by misstating the number of programs that they started with and pocketing the money for them on the side. For example, if you said that you had 25 programs, but it was actually 30, you had the opportunity to make $10 additional dollars. It was not my modus operandi—I never believed in stealing from anybody—but I always knew the score with some of my peers. Once everybody and the programs were accounted for, we received about $10 dollars to make change and the number of programs that you could comfortably carry.

It was always exciting to be in the stadium watching the players warm up when the stands were partially empty. And then it would happen: It was like floodgates opening, and people would sweep into the stadium, filling it up quickly, because nobody wanted to miss kick off or the Sonic Boom's entrance. Folks would be imitating the drum majors and dance line moves. Little kids would imitate the trombone and tuba players movements. Then, the sea of blue and white pompoms shook in concert with the sound of the band. Every fan on their feet as the Sonic Boom made its grand entrance.

If Jackson State was not playing Grambling, Southern University, or Mississippi Valley State University, it was not a good business decision to sell programs. Neither were the contests with Texas Southern and Prairie View, which didn't offer much opportunity to make money because the city did not really turn out for those games. After we received our programs, we raced throughout the stadium.

The spectators were well-intentioned, but trifling would be the best word to describe the Black fans I encountered in those days. They would pull some nonsense on us gullible teenagers. I'd be walking up and down concrete steps, shouting "Programs! Programs! Programs!" when a patron would summon me. After I trudged up several steps to get there, the first question was always, "How much the program cost?" When I said, "Two dollars," the moans and groans about how that's too much money started.

Sometimes I would allow a fan to preview one, but that was always a mistake. He would pass the program down the row and return it to me and not buy it. Now, if everyone seated on the row had pitched in .25 cents, they could easily have purchased the program, but not these trifling fans. I realized how naïve I was, but it would have been nice for them to give a kid a break. Then, there'd be someone who had too much to drink and was trying to be a comedian. All in all, I had my hands full.

The one game I always loved to work was the one with the Southern University Jaguars. They had the best Black college fans in the world. They traveled in carloads from Baton Rouge for the Jackson State game and always made you feel like family. We never had enough programs those evenings. Whole rows would buy a program, one for each spectator, and many of the women would recognize our efforts and give us a tip. I always made a couple of extra nickels those nights.

Here is how my friend Carlos Leach, who grew up on Jackson State football but ended up playing for Southern University from 1993 to 1997, remembers those games (he is now the managing partner at his law firm):

> *My experience as a player for the Southern University was like no other. During the 1990s, the rivalry between Jackson State and Southern University was at its most intense. This was because Jackson State was a formidable opponent with several championships that earned it the title "Mack of the SWAC." Every team was gunning to shatter the spirit of Tiger invincibility. So, for a kid like me who grew up on Jackson State Tiger football, playing for the hated rival (Southern) was quite a treat. Many of my family members and friends were in attendance for those games. At that time, Southern's caravan of fans was #1. An hour before kickoff, the stands would surge from 30,000 to 65,000 rowdy SWAC fans, with the sweet sounds of the Human Jukebox playing in the background. Then came the highlight of the day. The Sonic Boom of the South marched in led by the J-Settes and the bold sound of "Get Ready." It was the ultimate experience during football Saturdays in the SWAC. There was no better atmosphere, period!*

I learned a lot about responsibility, people, and money during those years, although I never knew how our efforts contributed to the university, booster club, or athletic department. It's funny how you can support something and don't see the fruits of your labor. Now, when I attend a Black College Football game, I always buy a program because it takes me back to that time and I think it's the right thing to do. BCF attendees should note the efforts and generosity of the Southern fans. It is important to reciprocate between schools because as the saying goes, "We all we got." It is not enough to buy a ticket to the game; supporting concessions and buying programs matter just as much.

I know we want to see where our money is going before we just give it away, but this money is important to the culture. There is nothing wrong with rivalry and passion for your team, but there must be economic compassion for fellow Black colleges, too. This is how fans and alums contribute to the quality of Black College Football. If people have a pleasant experience, they will offer support and spread the word. Through the years, I always took it on the chin quietly as a sidewalk Jackson State alum, because the Tigers never beat my real alma mater, Hampton University, in the three games they played from 2004 to 2008.

On October 31, 1987, the University of Southern Mississippi Golden Eagles played Jackson State on their home turf in Hattiesburg. This was an historic event because it was the first time one of the Mississippi Big Three (USM, Ole Miss and Mississippi State) played an HBCU. The Golden Eagles were quarterbacked by a young Brett Farve who would later star in the NFL, winning Superbowl XXXI with the Green Bay Packers. Jackson State brought its stars as well, namely running back Lewis Tillman and stalwart defender Darion Conner. Both Blue Bengals would play in the NFL as well. I did not attend this game. The Eagles defeated the Blue Bengals 17-7.

On August 31, 2002, Jackson State played the University of Southern Mississippi again. I was home on vacation, so I made the trek south to Hattiesburg by myself, decked out in a blue polo shirt to support my team. That year Jackson State had quarterback, Robert Kent, a force in the SWAC during his tenure. But it was not to be. The Golden eagles beat the Blue Bengals soundly, 55-7. As I left M.M. Roberts Stadium (aka The Rock), I received a lot of jeers from the locals. They did not really threaten anyone, but the message was clear: go back up the highway to Jackson. Funny thing, Hattiesburg could be considered Jackson South because of the number of Jackson Public School graduates that go there. USM played Jackson State again in 2018 and was scheduled to play them for 2020 season before COVID struck.

I merely provide these bits of history as background for a larger issue. USM administrators could take the lead and set an example for other colleges and universities. Why not play the game in Jackson? It is the state capital, and Veterans Stadium has more capacity than M.M. Roberts Stadium. I am not sure why it's called "The Rock," but it's not very spectator friendly. Depending on kickoff, if you are the visiting team, you just might spend the whole game squinting into the sun.

I understand the convenience for Eagle fans to have the game in their "backyard," but what about supporters of the Tigers? Kudos to USM's athletic department for making this contest between a PWI and HBCU happen, but let's take it a step further and have Jackson State host a game. It would save its athletic department some money and not make it seem like they're doing the Blue Bengals a favor. Besides, there are plenty of USM alums that live in Jackson.

Message to PWIs: Thank you for scheduling games with HBCUs, but you can do a lot more, and you should.

Mississippi Veterans Memorial Stadium was opened in 1950. Because of segregation, Historically Black Colleges and Universities were not allowed to play there. The first time I heard about an HBCU game held there was during Michelle Obama's 2016 commencement address to Jackson State. On October 21, 1967, Jackson State and Grambling integrated Veterans Stadium. Jackson State upset Grambling 20-14, a rare occasion, because the Grambling Tigers personify Black College Football like no other team.

Chapter 3

GRAMBLING

The will to win, desire to succeed, the urge to reach your full potential...these are the keys that will unlock the door to personal excellence.

— Coach Eddie Robinson

My aim in this book is not to profile every Historically Black College or University that fields a football team, or to offer a history lesson, but I want to highlight the contributions of Louisiana's Grambling State University to the sport. Grambling has probably given more not only to Black College Football but to the game itself than many other colleges. Eddie Robinson's legacy as a coach is second to none. He epitomizes what it means to prepare players regardless of their circumstances. He coached at Grambling for 57 seasons with a record of 408 wins, 165 losses and 15 ties.

Grambling has supplied the NFL with more talent than any other HBCU. In 1963, Junious "Buck" Buchanan was the first player drafted number one overall from a HBCU. Until now, he has been the only one. It happened because of Coach Robinson's vision and coaching prowess. When he retired in 1997 and no longer patrolled the sidelines, the G-Men fell on hard times. This happened to my beloved Blue Bengals, too, when legendary coach W. C. Gorden stepped away from the game.

Grambling matters to me personally because it's the only team I watched play in a Southwestern Athletic Conference (SWAC) stadium. I cannot recall the exact date, but it had to be 1990 or 1991. My dad and I headed to Grambling for the game with Jackson State. I can probably count the number of times on one hand that just my dad and I did that. When I played sports, he hardly ever attended any games because he was always working. As I recall, he made it to one baseball game when I was in the 9th grade. My Dad is a truck driver and a Vietnam Veteran. He is all about killing two birds with one stone—like hauling freight and looking up a family member in one trip to make it worth the effort. He always made sure I had what I needed when it came to school and sports, so I never took offense at his absences. I figured he had to be on the road to provide for the family. But the Grambling game was a special occasion—being able to spend time with my dad alone.

My Mom did not work due to a disability. On that Saturday, we hopped in Dad's silver Toyota pick-up and headed to Grambling via I-20 West. We were traveling along his usual route to Monroe, Louisiana, where he delivered his cargo for Saia LTL Freight. It's 155 miles from Jackson to Grambling. I never sleep much when traveling, so I was up and awake right along with him, talking a hole in his head most of the way.

We arrived at the stadium just in time for kickoff. I was disappointed that the Sonic Boom of the South was not in the stands. Jackson State's football team was dead on the field that night. The players had no life or energy. Half-time comes around and there was still no Sonic Boom, so we had to endure Grambling's band for the entire half-time show.

Then, out of nowhere, a tuba started blaring, and the Sonic Boom launched into its signature song, "Get Ready," by the Temptations and entered Eddie G. Robinson's stadium with all its glory and swagger. I get chills whenever the band plays that song. It makes me want to shout out loud, and there's no way I can sit still. It was the thrill of game for me. I don't remember if the Blue Bengals won that night, but I know their playing improved. It was like the band breathed new life into the football team.

My dad did not attend college, so I'm not sure why we went to this particular football game. Knowing him, I suspect it served as an alibi for a rendezvous with someone of the female persuasion. I benefited twice, like my dad (killing two birds with one stone). It was good to spend time with him, and I was thrilled that I was able to watch my Jackson State Tigers.

* * *

In the fall of 1999, I was stationed at Aberdeen Proving Grounds, Maryland, for my basic officer course training. I decided to attend the Whitney M. Young Classic at the Meadowlands in New Jersey. I had a black 1996 Nissan Sentra and drove by myself. Back then, there was no GPS, just directions from the Internet, but I had no trouble getting there. The game featured—you guessed it— Grambling State facing off against Hampton University. I don't remember the score, but any time I attend a classic, I buy a shirt or a program. I purchased my signature Tee-shirt and hit the road for Aberdump, as we (not so affectionately) called Aberdeen. I still have the shirt.

The following fall, Jackson State was schedule to play Southern University in New Orleans. I'm not sure how I got tickets, but I did not want to drive from Killeen, Texas—I was stationed at Fort Hood by then—to New Orleans by myself. I thought I had co-pilot, but he backed out on me at the last minute, and I was sorely disappointed. It probably was for the best, though, because I would go to these games and return home the same evening. No hotels, just turns and burns.[1]

I met my wife Athena at Fort Hood in the summer of 2000. At the time, I was the only African American commissioned officer in the battalion. A white female colleague told me about a black female officer that had been assigned to Charlie Company and thought she was cute. One day, I called the company headquarters where Athena worked and I asked her on a date. It was on a blind whim—I had not laid eyes on her. She did not know anything about me either, but the other female service members vouched for me, and she said yes. The rest is history—17 years and counting.

Athena attended Mercer University in Macon, Georgia, a predominantly white institution (PWI), and I thought it would be cool to expose her to the Black College Football experience. It had to be our third or fourth date when I invited her to accompany me to the Cotton Bowl Classic which featured Prairie View A&M versus Grambling. For me, there would be the added benefit of having someone with me on my crazy excursion. Athena obliged me and we made the 160-mile trek via I-35. The Texas State Fair was happening at the same time, and there were folks everywhere enjoying the food, rides, concession stands and other vendors. We had some time to kill before kickoff, so we walked around the fair grounds. I test drove a Buick Regal at a Buick vendor, and Athena had a picture

---

[1] Originally military jargon, referring to the moment after an aircraft drops its bombs, when the pilot turns quickly and shifts to after-burn to head home. Now also used by truck drivers.

taken of herself with a life-size cut-out of Tiger Woods. Then, we made our way into the stadium.

Nobody sits exactly according to the ticket seat numbers. You find a comfortable spot and set up shop. Athena wasn't a big football fan, so she didn't pay much attention to the game, while I followed the play-by-play intensely. That changed at halftime when Prairie Views' band came out to perform and Athena perked right up. I was biased because I believed, and still do, that the Sonic Boom is the baddest band in the land. True, Southern University's band, the Human Jukebox, deserves recognition because it displays the half-time score of each game and deserves credit for their preparation. But I had no idea what we were in for. When Prairie View's Marching Storm came out with six drum majors, my jaw dropped. I ran through my mental Rolodex to remember if I'd ever seen anything like it—six drum majors! Athena and I were fixated on them for the whole performance. Prairie View's band earned my respect and admiration that night. Prairie View's football team is another story because it was always a SWAC and NCAA cellar dweller, losing 80 games in a row. That year, Grambling whooped them 47-7. It wasn't until nine years later that Prairie View finally ended its long streak of losing, beating Alabama A&M to capture the SWAC championship.

Athena and I married in December 2003. It was not a part of our vows, but she knew what she was getting into in regard to my passion for HBCUs and football. She tolerates it and supports it with a good sense of humor.

Though I am not a Grambling alum, I have sidewalk alum tendencies with them, too. Coach Eddie Robinson and Doug Williams aside, I have enjoyed seeing Grambling play in a lot of games. That's why the team matters to me. I was delighted when in

1998, the year after Eddie Robinson retired, Grambling's number one son returned home to coach his alma mater. Just a reminder, Doug Williams was the first Black quarterback to win a Super Bowl and the MVP award, starring in Super Bowl XXII in which the Washington Redskins defeated the Denver Broncos 42-10. When I was growing up, Mom always said, "Root for the Black coach and quarterback," so I have been partial to Redskins football, as well as Georgetown University basketball because of Coach John Thompson. During Coach Williams' first stint at Grambling from 1998-2003, he quickly returned the school to its former glory by winning the SWAC championship in 2000 and 2001.

When Coach Williams departed soon after, becoming a personnel executive with the Tampa Bay Buccaneers, he did not leave the cupboard bare because the Tigers won the championship again in 2005 under Coach Melvin Spears. It seemed that Coach Williams had left the team on course, heading in the right direction.

As life would have it, I was stationed at Fort Lewis, now Joint Base Lewis-McChord, south of Tacoma, Washington, from 2004 to 2008. On September 17, 2005, Grambling traveled to Seattle to take on Washington State University. The game took place at Qwest Field, now Century Link Field, home to the Seattle Seahawks. A Black College Football team in the Pacific Northwest! Of course, I had to go. There was no way I was going to miss this event even though I did not think Grambling had a chance to win the game and managed my expectations accordingly. I left around the third quarter because the game was not competitive. The final score was 48-7. A fellow Army officer who attended the game with me and did not know much about Black College Football or Grambling's history was sorely disappointed. I don't recall an HBCU returning to the Pacific Northwest during my tour of duty there. Washington

State was in no hurry to travel to Louisiana for a rematch. Still, as I mentioned earlier, Grambling captured the SWAC championship that year.

When Doug Williams returned to Grambling for a second stint in 2011, he picked up where he left off and won the SWAC title in his first year back. But two years later at the beginning of the 2013 season, he was abruptly fired. I was dumbfounded. According to Coach Williams, he was let go for raising money for the football team outside the "administration's purview." As far as I was concerned, it was a lame excuse. If Coach Williams was not doing anything illegal or unethical to bring shame to the university, there was no justification for his removal. Heck, he is Mr. Grambling every year. I don't care who gets the sash and crown at the annual ceremony, but I don't know how you can treat your most illustrious alum in that manner. The school's president could have at least waited until the end of the season.

Politics between coaches and university presidents play a big role in college football, but it is usually boosters who try to get rid of a coach. Nobody cares who the President of the University of Alabama is, except his family, but fans know Coach Nick Saban. In fact, boosters wouldn't give their ace away, definitely not someone like Mr. Grambling. Coach Williams recruited well and raised money for the program and, most importantly, he was winning.

Then, to make matters worse, on October 19, 2013, the Grambling football players refused to travel to Jackson to play Jackson State for its homecoming game. They claimed their boycott was about deplorable locker room conditions. I'm sure the facilities had been subpar for the past several years, but I refused to believe that 2013 marked the first year that they were not up to standard. More likely, the boycott was due to Coach Williams being fired.

I hated what happened to my Blue Bengals, and not just the disappointed players and fans. Homecoming games bring revenue to cities. Everyone benefits from ticket sales, greater hotel occupancy, club events, and restaurant attendance. All the anticipation and preparations were for nothing.

I have heard of individual players boycotting games, but not an entire team. This had to be a first and the fact that it was a Black College Football team only made it worse, in my estimation. Optics matter. And so does money. The average college fan recognizes Grambling because of Eddie Robinson's legacy. But in this day and age, HBCUs are underfunded, and their athletic departments even more so. In the early 1900s, the schools would send choirs and bands around the nation to raise money. That is no longer the case, and nothing has replaced those fund-raising efforts. So, if there are no plans to invest in the football programs, the colleges and universities should not have teams. College football serves as the foundation for the other athletic programs. At more successful schools, the revenue from college football supports the less popular sports, such as bowling and lacrosse. At most HBCUs, football does not generate enough money to fund other sports.

As for Grambling's 2013 boycott, I blamed the SWAC conference's leadership. The conference should have known the state of athletic facilities for its members' schools. There should be an emergency fund or financing available to assist schools with safety and quality issues.

Instead Grambling forfeited the game. That was no consolation for all the Jackson State alums who had made plans to attend the homecoming festivities and game only to find out a few days before that the game was canceled. No football teams. No fans. No bands. Constructively, Jackson State played a short scrimmage that fans could attend for free, but that was small consolation.

Despite the turmoil, Grambling's football program recovered, remained competitive, and captured back to back SWAC championships in 2016 and 2017. I continue to be a big fan and appreciate the positive impact the team has made on my family.

My youngest daughter, Camille, loves the Dancing Dolls. The organization trains young men and women to compete in dance team competitions across the nation. The team has a television show, *Bring It* that airs on Lifetime TV. During one episode, they visited the Grambling State campus. My 11-year-old daughter, wants to be a member of the Dancing Dolls, so when she saw that show, she decided that she wanted to go to Grambling. I have been trying to tell her that the school is in the Louisiana woods, but it doesn't matter to her. If Grambling is good enough for the Dancing Dolls, it's good enough for her.

Finally, Grambling is the only HBCU with a TV movie to its credit. *Grambling's White Tiger*, which aired 1981, tells the true story of Jim Gregory, the first white quarterback at Grambling. Harry Belafonte played Coach Robinson.

Let's recap Grambling's achievements. Its football team can point to the first HBCU player drafted number one overall in NFL draft, a Super Bowl winning quarterback, an all-time, winningest Coach in BCF, and a TV Movie! If Grambling is not the epitome of Black College Football, I don't know what is!

Chapter 4

HAMPTON

You didn't choose Hampton. Hampton chose you.
—Dr. William Harvey
President of Hampton University

I attended Hampton University and graduated spring of 1999. During my freshman year, the school, which considers itself the real HU—a jab at Howard University, for those of you not familiar with the rivalry—was transitioning from the Central Intercollegiate Athletic Association (CIAA) to the Mid-Eastern Atlantic Conference (MEAC). Hampton's football team, the Pirates, had dominated the CIAA under Coach Joe Taylor's leadership, so it seemed fitting to jump from Division II to Division I-AA.

Now, I am SWAC man to my core, always have been, always will be, and I had to adjust to MEAC football. Just becoming familiar with the other schools in the conference was a bit of a challenge. I didn't know any of the songs the MEAC schools' bands were performing either. But during my time at Hampton, I never missed a home game. I was there for kickoff and would stay the whole game. My homeboys and I would talk about every game like we were on *First Take*, critiquing the players, dissecting plays and discussing the outcomes. A couple of them were sports management majors, which I thought meant gym majors—what did I know!—and they were more familiar with the athletes throughout our time at Hampton than I was.

During the transition to the MEAC, the football team moved away from a Wing-T-style offense to a more pro-style offense. The Wing-T was primarily a misdirection, rushing attack, whereas the pro-style offense utilized both passing and rushing, depending on defensive alignment. For its first year in the new conference, the team's record was 8-3. The most notable game that season was a familiar SWAC foe, Southern University. Southern beat us badly with a score of 45-22. In 1996, my sophomore year, Hampton's record was 5-6. There was no signature win that year. But the following year, we were schedule to play William & Mary, the second oldest institution of higher learning in the United States, in a home and home series (where the away team acts as host the following year). The first game took place in Williamsburg, so my homeboys and I made the 30-mile trek via I-64 West to Zable Stadium to support our team. Boy, were the Pirates outmatched that game. The Tribe beat us 31-6. William & Mary had a white receiver reminiscent of Wes Welker, who had his way with our defensive backs that afternoon. HU defenders could not cover that guy for nothing.

For a team like Hampton, games against a respected PWI provide a good benchmark. It's all fine and dandy to dominate HBCU competition, but, ultimately, wins against other teams are important to a program's progress and reputation. The 1997 football team finished the season 10-2 and ultimately lost to Youngstown State in the FCS playoffs. The 1998 campaign was probably the toughest year for me as an alum, but I will get to that later.

That year, William & Mary had to come to our house aka "Our Home By The Sea" as Hampton is affectionately called. In 1998, the university president invested a significant amount of money into the stadium. There was a new scoreboard with video replay. Like HU alums say, "It's just different at Hampton." No other HBCU had anything like it at that time. Anyhow, that game was probably the best college contest I have ever watched in person. It was like a heavyweight fight. William & Mary delivered a blow, and Hampton countered. HU delivered a blow, and William & Mary responded. It was back and forth like that all game long. The previous year's ass-whipping they put on us at Zable Stadium was not lost on our team or the fans—to us it was like "Remember the Alamo." I was never prouder to be a Hamptonian. I even forgot about my beloved Jackson State that day.

In the 4th quarter, the game was tied 34-34. William & Mary's wide receiver was not the Wes Welker from a year ago, but an African American player. The HU defensive back covered him man to man and was all over him. On a comeback route, the Tribe's receiver caught the ball and our defender hit him immediately. The play happened lightning fast, and it looked like the Tribe receiver's butt cheek touched the grid iron at the same time as he put his hand down. The HU defender assumed that he'd done his job. But there was no whistle, and the Tribe receiver played through the contact and ran for the score. Touchdown: William & Mary! The HU sideline went ballistic, as did the fans. Hampton's president even came out of the press box and onto the sideline. The scoreboard played it over and over, showing clearly: the receiver's ass kissed the turf.

Clearly, the referee missed the call, but there was still time on the clock. The university president was irate. Coach Taylor seemed to manage his emotions. The 1998 team was a good team, and it was time to strap up! HU's offense had been moving the ball on the Tribe all day, but emotions got the better of the team that day.

They lost focus and could not rebound. Ultimately, the Pirates fell to the Tribe 41-34.

All anybody could talk about was that play. A lot of us thought that it was racism on the part of the referee, favoring the white team, even if there were black players on the roster. I found an article in the *Daily Press* that acknowledged the game as a "controversy." I also did not realize that the officials at the game had been suspended by the MEAC commissioner for the missed call, so it really was not Black versus White, despite all appearances. Heck, the referees were from the MEAC conference.

The 1998 Hampton team made the playoffs that year but lost to Connecticut 42-34. At my last home game as an undergraduate, we lost homecoming to a raggedy Bethune-Cookman University team. I did not follow HU football much after that because I was commissioned as a Second Lieutenant in the U.S. Army. Finding my way in my new career, serving at different locations in the United States, and deploying to Afghanistan and Iraq kept me busy.

Coach Taylor stayed at HU for 16 years. His record was 136-48-1, which adds up to a 73.5 winning percentage. He even transitioned the team to from the CIAA to the MEAC, a considerable upgrade. During his tenure, several players were drafted into the NFL. But an alleged power struggle between him and the university president led to his departure in 2004. HU football has not done much since Coach Taylor left. 2006 was the last year HU appeared in the football playoffs.

This is one of the reasons that Black College Football struggles. I know booster support at HBCUs is not at the level of SEC schools, but the president should stay in his lane. When it comes to athletics, his job is to ensure the coach has what he needs to develop players and foster their abilities and character on and off the field. Beyond that, a hands-off approach is best, especially when a winning coach is not tied up in controversy. Winning is not easy; and sustaining success, even harder.

In 2019, I returned to Hampton University to celebrate the 20-year reunion with my classmates. If you want to tailgate, you must purchase a ticket to the game and to the tailgate area. This makes financial sense. It boosts ticket sales numbers and revenue. I complied, but I did not attend the game. I remained in the tailgate area. It did not matter to me who we played.; I just could not bring myself to sit through the game. HU had a marquee player, named Deondre Francois. He was the team's highly recruited starting quarterback who had transferred from Florida State. He is talented, and I am sure an upstanding young man, but to have to transfer from the Seminoles and land at HU? Deondre Francois was playing in front of 70,000 fans and on national television at Florida State. At Hampton, the largest crowd might have been 25,000, with local television coverage at best. Players transition from division I-A to I-AA all the time, but he was the starting quarterback for Florida State!

Isaiah Crowell is another player that comes to mind. He was a star running back at the University of Georgia and the Southeastern Conference's Freshman of the Year. Dismissed for violating team rules, he transferred to Alabama State.

Deondre Francois and Isaiah Crowell won't be the last players to be let go from big time college football programs because of foolish misbehavior and end up at an HBCU. It is a shame that they were too inexperienced to value their talents and take advantage of the opportunities they had. Moving from an elite program to a smaller school is akin to "slumming" or leaving caviar for chitterlings. Both players were touted as top National Football League prospects. Francois has yet to attain his NFL aspirations, but Crowell was signed by Cleveland Browns as an undrafted free agent in 2014. He has been a serviceable running back for two different teams, never rushing for a 1000 yards during a season. Currently, he is with the Las Vegas Raiders on injury reserve because of a torn Achilles. He will be a free agent next year.

A lot changed in the 20 years since I graduated from Hampton University, but the Pirate's football team's play has not measured up to its potential and former glory. I understand that nothing stays the same, but HU has the funds. In fact, it has more than average facilities for all its athletic programs.

On July 1, 2018, Hampton left the MEAC to join the Big South Conference, which was established in 1983 and is headquartered in Charlotte, North Carolina. The Big South Conference football programs consist of Campbell University, Charleston Southern, Gardner-Webb, Kennesaw State, Monmouth, North Alabama, and Presbyterian College. If HU had been a dominant team, as it was during its tenure in CIAA, I would be all for the move, but football at my alma mater has been average at best. That's not to say that the other athletic teams would not benefit from the move. In 1998 and 2004, HU shared the MEAC football championship. Then, the Pirates won the conference championship outright in 2005 and 2006. From 2004 to 2007, HU's football team was recognized as the three-time, SBN-Black College National Champion. During that time, the team was ranked in the top 25 of the Division I Football Championship Subdivision (FCS) poll each year. The Pirates sent five players to the NFL Combine in 2007, the most of any FCS school that year. But Hampton never won a playoff game against other conference champions during its time in the MEAC, a strong indicator that it wasn't ready to compete at a higher level.

Hampton is the second HBCU to join a non-Black conference. Tennessee State University has participated the Ohio Valley Conference since 1986. It took me several years to realize that TSU was not in the SWAC because it plays Jackson State in the Southern Heritage Classic in Memphis every year. It's an easy assumption that an HBCU would belong to a Black conference.

I don't understand Hampton's move. It is bad timing, in my opinion. But money makes the world go round, and the university's leadership justified its decision to leave the MEAC on economic grounds. Now, the football team does not have to go as far for its games, significantly reducing travel expenses.

But here's the reality. None of the Big South football teams have fared any better than MEAC football teams when it comes to playoff success or championships. I reviewed Hampton's 2020 schedule, and there are two Division II teams on the slate. I thought this was the purpose of leaving the CIAA years ago: to compete against Division I level opponents. Chances are, HU football will be a cellar dweller in the Big South. The only thing the move assures is that, along with Tennessee State, there will be two HBCU teams that can win the FCS championship. Basically, a 2% chance. In 2019, HU went 5-7 for the season, with a signature loss to Virginia Union. More than 20 years ago, the Pirates left them behind in the CIAA because of our dominance, but now we cannot even compete with them.

It is a shame because there was a time when things were different, when Black College Football mattered.

Chapter 5

THE GOLDEN ERA OF STEVE "AIR II" MCNAIR

McNair is Black College Football.
—Jay "Sky" Walker

Everyone has their own idea about the Golden Era of a particular sport, music, movies, or television for that matter. Sometimes it's a personal thing, sometimes there is general agreement. For me, the Golden Era of Black College Football was 1991 to 1994. The time coincided with my coming of age in Jackson and Steve McNair playing college football for Alcorn State University in Mississippi. As I think back on all the games that I attended at Veterans Stadium, the most electrifying, and, in retrospect, most relevant, were the ones with McNair. He was nicknamed "Air McNair" for a reason. He was going to air it out all night, all over the field, until there were zeros on the time clock.

My first Black College Football game was Jackson State University versus Mississippi Valley State University, on September 22, 1984. In those days, BCF games would take place at night with kickoff around 7:30 pm, because there were times when Ole Miss or Mississippi State played a game earlier that day. We'd sit in the bleachers among the remnants of dipping and chewing tobacco, reminders that one or the other team had used the stadium.

By the way, the Egg Bowl, which featured Ole Miss and Mississippi State, was played at Veterans Stadium from 1973 to 1991. This was many moons before the development of the Grove in Oxford and before Starkville became Starkvegas. Ole Miss and Mississippi State have improved their facilities to the point that they will never entertain the thought of playing at Veterans stadium again. The stadium was never special in my view—brick, mortar, and stiff aluminum seats hard on your butt.

My first game was supposed to be a family event. Unfortunately, there was a mishap when my little cousin was playing in the street. Neither my cousin nor my neighbor was paying attention, and the neighbor's vehicle struck her. I cannot remember if my Dad took her to the hospital or if an ambulance was called. Fortunately, she was all right and suffered only a few scrapes. In the meantime, my Aunt Tricia T took my brother and me to the game.

In my neighborhood, some residents had gone to Valley State, others had attended Jackson State. That meant that some families had a house divided, which, I imagine, caused some changes in the homes leading up to the game. Like no one touching the other's game-day shirt, pompoms or school's flag. There would be no cooked meals, just TV dinners. Still, most couples sat together during the game, as this rivalry was not as extreme as the Alabama-Auburn contest. Usually, things returned to normal the following Monday regardless of who won the game.

At the time, I did not know that this would turn out to be a historic game. Not only did it set an attendance record with more than 64,000 people coming to watch—I was lucky to be one of them—but it also ended a long losing streak. Valley had not beaten Jackson State in 27 years! I was not familiar with the players on either team despite their notoriety, namely Jerry "World" Rice as wide receiver and Willie "Satellite" Totten as quarterback for Valley. All I knew was that Jackson State was not ready. The halftime score was 35-14. For a long time, I thought that was the final score, but it was actually 49-32. We did not have the heart to remain for the rest of the game, which is probably why 35-14 is etched in my memory. I felt dejected for my Blue Bengals—I mean sick to my stomach—all the way home.

A funny thing happened, though. I started rooting for the rival team's star players. I read up on Rice and Totten, followed their careers, and emulated them during our neighborhood football games. If I drew the quarterback slot, I imagined I was Willie Totten. Jerry Rice had a big towel hanging from his football pants, so when I played wide receiver, I would use a kitchen towel to get into my Rice character. The one fact I learned about Jerry Rice's upbringing that really impressed me was that his father was a mason and would throw bricks to him during the jobs. That is, supposedly, how Rice developed his catching ability. You can guess what happened next. Imagine some young adolescents tossing bricks at each other and trying to catch them. Bricks are heavy and if your hands are not tough you have no desire to squeeze the bricks like a football. Needless to say, that activity was short lived.

But it's no wonder that I am such a fan. I was virtually baptized into Black College Football history. I was eight years old when my Blue Bengals lost. But I also attended the "Game of the Century" in Mississippi when Valley faced off against Alcorn State University that same year. Originally, it was supposed to be played in Itta Bena, where Valley was located, but the demand for tickets was so great that the venue shifted 60 miles to the south, to our Veterans Stadium. The contest took place on November 4, 1984, which was a Sunday. Because it was such a big deal, the game was broadcast live on television as well. I went with both my parents and two of my uncles. One of them brought his binoculars with their case. The binoculars hung around his neck, but the case was draped over his shoulders and contained a liter of Crown Royal whiskey. In those days, no alcohol was sold at Veterans Stadium, so you had to smuggle it in.

The atmosphere in the stadium was electrifying, and the game was a hard-fought struggle, but in the end, the Alcorn Braves prevailed 42-28. The star of the game was Alcorn's defensive back, Isaac Holt. He was responsible for covering Jerry Rice that night. Rice caught eight passes for 134 yards and a touchdown. Those were good numbers but well below Rice's average for the year. Holt had a key interception, too, that he returned for a touchdown to seal the victory for the Braves.

After college, Holt played nine years in the NFL and won Super Bowl XXVII with the Cowboys. He was probably the only defensive back that had a decent game against Rice that year.

I have to admit that I couldn't follow much of the game and perhaps even fell asleep at some point, but I believe that the excitement rubbed off on me and solidified me as a life-long fan of Black College Football.

Besides the programs from games featuring HBCUs, I would always buy a team flag, so I had Alcorn, Jackson State, and Valley State pennants displayed on the wall in my room. As I started to appreciate the football games more, I made it a point to follow SWAC players that made it to the National Football League, especially Jerry Rice. He is my favorite wide receiver of all time despite what Odell Beckham Jr. may accomplish in the future. Which brings me back to Steve McNair.

You see, McNair never lost to my beloved Blue Bengals. I hated not beating Alcorn's Braves, but I always appreciated being in the stadium when he played; I knew he was going to put on a show. I don't think I ever saw him get sacked. His throws were missiles. When he released the ball, it would spin in razor-targeted spirals all over the field—short and deep, and to crossing route ends. But what I loved most about McNair was how he moved in the pocket. He probably could have rushed for 2000 yards every year, but I think running was always a last resort for him. Because of McNair's dominance of Jackson State, a SWAC championship was an afterthought because the road to the championship was through McNair.

During his last college season in 1994, he broke records and became the NCAA All-Time Leader in total offense, despite playing hurt a lot that year. ESPN followed every Alcorn game because McNair was getting closer to breaking the record with every game. Media vans camped out at Alcorn's campus, aka the Reservation, piping live feeds to their networks. McNair broke the record on October 22, 1994, against Southern University, and his Heisman campaign was in full swing. There was a song, shirts, and a big-time public relations campaign.

I was biding my time, knowing McNair was scheduled to play Valley in Jackson. The game took place on November 5, 1994. I was 17 years old and a senior in high school. Because of an increase in nighttime violence in Jackson, kickoff for the games now took place in the afternoon rather than in the evening. As I made my way to Veterans Stadium, I noticed a contingent of white fans, just a sprinkle, which further indicated what it meant to bear witness to

McNair's greatness. I was dating at the time, and my girlfriend was with me. Her dad had gone to Valley, and her mom had attended Jackson State, but she wanted to enroll in Alcorn. We found a good spot with a decent view. We could see McNair on the sideline with a wrap on his leg which confirmed a reported hamstring injury. He was in uniform but didn't wear his helmet.

This was only the second game that McNair did not start in four years at Alcorn. He came off the bench in 1991 as a freshman to lead a comeback victory against Grambling. The Braves could not get out of their own way on the first possession, or the next two. By then, either the head coach or McNair had seen enough. McNair trotted out on the field. I was happy to see him. On his first play, he lined up in the shot gun. When the ball was snapped, Valley had a good pass rush with a clear path to McNair. He side-stepped one opponent, then another, did a 360, stepped up in the pocket, and fired a laser. The receiver caught the ball for a first down. I could not imagine being one of McNair's receivers and not catching the ball, although it did happen once in a while. The most infamous drop was by Percy Singleton. In the first game of the 1994 season, Alcorn was trailing Grambling in the fourth quarter. On the final play, McNair let one rip into the end zone only to have the ball hit Singleton's hands and fall to the ground. But not this night. After that first play, the band was in full swing, playing the Brave chant with Alcornites in the stands performing the tomahawk chop. I can still hear and feel those moments. The Braves won 49-24, and McNair was dominant as always—even on only one good leg.

The finale that year was Jackson State versus Alcorn at the Capital City Classic on November 19, 1994. (I did not realize that the inaugural Classic had been played just a year before.) I had anticipated going to the game and be in the stands for quite some time, but my feelings were all in a jumble. I was happy McNair was leaving because that was our best chance to beat Alcorn, but I also experienced a sense of melancholy because this would be the last time, I could be that close, that intimate with McNair. We lost 52-34, but I cheered for McNair on the inside and really appreciated him that day. I don't recall any special, signature plays from that afternoon. I just know that my Blue Bengals lost, and this was the last time that McNair would play in the SWAC.

No player has thrilled me as much since then, and I spend more time in the tailgate area and supporting vendors than I care about the outcome of the games I attend. Nothing compares to the way I feel about Jerry Rice as an all-time great, or the way I endorse Steve McNair as my GOAT—Greatest Of All Time HBCU player. I know other fine players preceded him, and some may come in the future, and it would be wonderful to experience again the electricity that McNair generated inside a stadium. In support of his GOAT campaign, you should understand the following elements: He finished third in the Heisman voting his final year, which is the highest for any Black college player. His stats were outstanding; his will to win was extraordinary. Most importantly, Alcorn always had a chance for victory when McNair was the quarterback. He was going to put up points, and he was not going to stop scoring until there were zeros on the clock.

Also, during McNair's time, Alcorn was probably the most competitive an HBCU had been against predominantly white institutions. In 1994, Alcorn played four PWIs (Chattanooga, Samford, Troy, and Sam Houston State) during the regular season. The Braves went 2-1-1. They beat Chattanooga and Troy, lost at Sam Houston State (48-23), and tied at Samford 45-45. Alcorn made the playoffs but lost to Youngstown State 63-20. The game took place in Ohio. Youngstown State was the previous year's champion and went on to win the championship again in 1994 under Coach Jim Tressel. As an aside, Coach Tressel moved on to Ohio State and restored the football team there to dominance in the Big 10.

I know if that game had been played at Veterans Stadium, the outcome would have been different. Yes, Youngstown had more talent as a whole, but imagine what McNair would have done with that southern atmosphere and fans rooting for him instead of playing in the cold, grim Midwest.

Finally, I would be remiss if I did not acknowledge Jay "Sky" Walker, who starred at Howard University for the 1992 and 1993 seasons and was a prolific passer in his own right. In 1993, he out-dueled McNair 38-36 and led Howard to an undefeated season. He was drafted to the NFL in 1994. Jay Walker is now an ESPN analyst. He broadcasts a lot of Black College football games and currently serves his community as a Maryland State delegate. He represents what's best about BCF because of his play on the field and his life after football. He competed against McNair and is responsible for the quote at the beginning of this chapter: "McNair is Black College Football."

Chapter 6

HBCU CLASSICS

We are caught in an inescapable network of mutuality, tied in a single garment of destiny. Whatever affects one directly affects all indirectly.

—Martin Luther King, Jr.

HBCU classics are an opportunity to showcase the essence of Black College Football. The fierce competition on the gridiron, the spectacular marching bands, and the dazzling dance line girls. And above all, the fans, the people in the stands. What clothing styles are on display? Most people wear their team colors, while some folks sport their Sunday best—clean from head to toe. Classics also serve as an opportunity to recruit prospective students that might not have considered attending a HBCU. Most southern states have classics, but the objective is to hold the games in places where there are plenty of Black folks but no HBCUs.

The Whitney M. Young Classic, arguably the first HBCU classic, was established in 1971. The game featured Maryland's Morgan State University versus Grambling State University. It was played at Yankee Stadium and televised live. I think it's fitting that Grambling is one of the teams, having been the standard of excellence for BCF for years. In 1987, the annual contest was relocated from Yankee Stadium to New Jersey. I attended the 1999 Whitney M. Young Classic there. Hampton defeated Grambling 27-7. I don't have any memorable recollections from the game. I went just to be able to say I was there and left right after halftime to return to Aberdeen Proving Ground to continue my officer training. The event has been since renamed the New York Urban League Classic.

The Circle City Classic was established in 1984. The game is played in Indianapolis at Lucas Oil Stadium. The Chicago Classic was established in 1997. It has been contested for over 20 years at Soldier Field.

I highlight these three classics because they have been promoting BCF for years. I have never attended the Chicago Classic or the Circle City Classic. However, for them to still be around after so many years displays these cities' commitment to support and host these games. Notice, I did not mention the Bayou Classic, which I consider to be a state classic; that is, a game played between two schools from the same state. The Bayou Classic will always feature Grambling and Southern, while the others have different matchups each year.

On October 28, 2011, I traveled the 150 miles from Columbus, Georgia, via U.S. 280 to Birmingham. I was driving my blue F-150 pick-up truck aka, Blu Mag!c. My first Magic City Classic was the 70th meeting between Alabama A&M and Alabama State. K. Rich had been after me for some time to come to the classic. Also, two good friends of mine are alums of these two fine institutions Dre (ASU) and Mo (A&M), and they always talk up their respective schools.

I arrived on Friday night to attend an all-black party at the Sheraton and gauge the atmosphere of downtown Birmingham before calling it a night. Saturday afternoon, K. Rich picked me up and we headed to the legendary Legion Field.

Opening in 1927, and named in honor of the American Legion, the stadium hosted the final game of the regular season between Alabama and Auburn from 1948 to 1988, also known as the Iron Bowl because of Birmingham's iron and steel manufacturing industry. It used to have an upper deck with "Football Capital of the South" displayed on its facade, which was removed in 2004. Since then, the stadium has seating for more than 70,000 people.

I have been to a lot of Black College Football games, but I could not get over the number of Black folks that were in attendance. They filled the entire stadium, and their excitement was infectious. I felt at ease like I was at a family reunion. The only thing that bothered me was to see spectators dressed in apparel from other HBCUs than were playing. I believe people should follow HBCU football etiquette. When I attend classics, I never sport my Hampton colors. I think it's disrespectful to wear one's alma mater's gear at a HBCU classic where other teams are playing. To me, it's like planting a flag on someone else's turf just to show off. If you must put your colors on, I don't think you're supporting the classic. I get the notion of supporting family members or friends, but putting on your colors is not the way to do it. Leave them at home.

Myself, I was wearing an LSU football jersey. Considering I was in Alabama, it was not the best choice. Here I was, in Roll Tide country ("Roll Tide Roll" is the rallying cry of Alabama's Crimson Tide's athletic teams), wearing gear of an archenemy in the Southeastern Conference. I received a lot of jeers and side-eyes that night.

The game was a squeaker—A&M won 20-19—but I was most impressed by the show the Greeks put on. When I was in college, I did not pledge a fraternity, but I have to salute the Divine Nine, the umbrella organization that represents the nine Black Greek letter societies. I have seen a lot of step shows and probate shows through the years, but I had never witnessed a Greek organization perform as hard as the Omegas at the Magic City Classic. I mean, these cats strolled and hopped from 10 a.m. to 10 p.m. The only breathers they got were when the stroll songs slowed down and reduced their pace. I watched for a good hour, bopping along. It was impossible not to have a good time.

On my drive back to Columbus, I thought about whether the Magic was the premier BCF classic and nicknamed it the Eighth Wonder of the World.

In the summer of 2013, the Army reassigned me to Joint Base Lewis McChord, southwest of Tacoma, Washington. For two years, there would be no Magic City Classic or Black College Football for me. Washington is an outstanding place to live, and the assignment was first rate, but without BCF it felt like purgatory. During that time, I would call up K. Rich just to find out which classics he was going to and to get his thorough account of the festivities and the game. As fate and fortune would have it, in the summer 2015, the Army relocated me to Columbus, Georgia. I was excited to be back in the South to support and enjoy Black College Football.

In 2016, I declared that I was going to attend as many classics as my schedule would allow. Fortunately, two of them—the Tiger Classic and Fountain City—were played in Columbus, Georgia. I already knew I was going to the Magic City Classic. It was my 15th Hampton reunion and I made sure to book HU's homecoming. But the first classic that I attended that year was the 5th Quarter

Classic featuring Florida A&M and Tuskegee University. At the time, I did not know that Tuskegee (668) and FAMU (574) are number one and two for all-time wins among HBCUs.

The game was played on September 17, 2016 in Mobile, Alabama, at Ladd-Pebbles Stadium. Named in honor of Ernest Ladd, a local banking tycoon, it opened in 1948. Nearly 50 years later, in 1997, it was renamed Ladd-Pebbles to also honor civic leader E.B. Pebbles for his efforts to enhance the Senior Bowl experience. The Senior Bowl has been played there since 1951. In 2008, the University of South Alabama added football and started playing at the stadium the following year. I was looking forward to checking out Ladd-Pebbles because it hosts the Senior Bowl for future NFL prospects.

I also picked this game because I had a homeboy in Mobile, and it would be a good opportunity to spend time with him. Another homeboy of mine lived in Enterprise, Alabama. He had never experienced a Black College Football game, so I took a circuitous route to pick him up.

One of the challenging things about attending any football event is where to park. For that game night, we parked at a church where the parishioners assured us that nothing was going to happen to my truck.

As we approached the stadium on foot, the atmosphere was vibrant with excitement, but not as much as it could have been. Unfortunately, it was raining, not hard but enough to deter some people from attending. Black folks don't do rainy events; people were huddled inside the stadium in covered areas to get out of the rain. The stadium is not a horseshoe, so you had to walk all the way down and around to get to the other side. We didn't stay long. Heck, we even skipped the halftime show.

When I returned to the hotel, some older FAMU alums were hanging out in the lobby. Joining their conversation, I learned that they lost 20-17 to TU. True, Tuskegee is a worthy opponent, but a much smaller school, and only Division II. I guess, FAMU's football team could not get out of its own way that day. As we conversed, a gentleman mentioned that FAMU administrators were misallocating his donations. His six-figure gift was not going to the department it was earmarked for, and he was not getting any response from the university when he asked about it. That led to more than an hour discussion about the state of Black College Football. We concluded that our game faced some challenging times, but now was not the time for our support to waiver.

I always enjoy these conversations with older alums and appreciate gaining their perspective. It seems that most members of the generation after me could care less about Black College Football. It might not be fair to criticize them so soon, but they need to know the history of BCF and the importance of supporting the games whenever they can. Because the United States elected Barack Obama as the first African American president, some pundits suggested that it represented a shift to a post-racial society. Clearly, that has yet to happen, as so many ugly, recent events have demonstrated.

Nonetheless, some people feel that HBCUs are no longer necessary, even though prior to integration, they were the only college institutions that educated Black folks. That's why the legacy of Black College Football is important. I hope BCF's fate does not go the way of Negro League Baseball which has become a myth in many people's minds because no one kept the memory alive. Only a couple of places pay homage to the forgotten baseball pioneers. Jackie Robinson and Satchel Paige were not the only players to star in the Negro League, but if you don't study history, you would believe they were the only good players.

Next up, October 8, 2016 was the Tiger Classic, Tuskegee versus Morehouse. I'm partial to TU because of its founder, Booker T. Washington, arguably Hampton's most illustrious alum (besides yours truly). Thus, I am a TU sidewalk alum. The game is played at A. J. McClung Memorial Stadium, which is basically a high school venue. As the third oldest stadium in Georgia, it hosted the "Deep South's Oldest Rivalry" from 1916 to 1958, featuring Auburn University versus the University of Georgia. As for the stadium's namesake, Arthur Joseph "A.J." was active in advancing civil rights in Columbus. In 1973, he served as the first African American mayor for Columbus. The first game of the Tuskegee-Morehouse rivalry dates to 1935 when it provided entertainment for the local population and African American service members assigned to Fort Benning. For this classic, I didn't go inside the stadium but enjoyed the tailgate activities. Although attendance was modest, I noticed a lot of older alums supporting their respective alma maters.

The next week, I took a flight to Hampton for my 15th reunion. When you attend homecoming, you don't care about the game. You go to reconnect with old friends and recall the good old days on campus. Returning to Hampton, especially when my closest classmates have come as well, is always a good time. The campus bazaar, parties, and tailgating were all quality events. I just mentioned this trip to depict how much traveling I did this particular year.

From October 28 to 30, I was in Birmingham for the Magic City classic. The game marked the 75th meeting between Alabama A&M and Alabama State. My friend Dre, an ASU alum, was getting married in July 2017, so I bought the commemorative painting for his wedding gift, which depicts two older, African American gentlemen playing chess. They are adorned in their respective school colors, and the room features memorabilia from both schools. I described my first Magic City Classic experience earlier, and it never disappoints. I enjoy the events and the atmosphere. I am always observant of any significant changes from year to year. Most importantly, I get to hang out with K. Rich. That time, I did not even go inside the game. Who said I don't support my HBCUs?

On November 5, 2016, I went to the Fountain City Classic (Albany State versus Fort Valley State). Since it takes place in Columbus, I did not have to travel far. The tailgate action and attendance turned out to be livelier than the Tiger Classic itself. It was probably due to the proximity of both schools and the fact that there are more Fountain City alums living in Columbus, so I made my rounds. Some folks were dressed to the tee, others just wore comfortable clothes. There were vendors hustling their wares— team paraphernalia, music CDs, T-shirts, and other garments. The city of Columbus always gives a little leeway for this game. There was the smell of weed in the air. Folks walking around publicly consuming liquor and beer out the bottle. Because Columbus is a military town, you're always going to run into a veteran or two. I ate my usual diet of fish and turkey legs. If I see any unique Greek paraphernalia, I grab something for Athena, who is a Delta.

Fort Valley defeated Albany State 21-17. I appreciate having a classic in my backyard. The reason that I don't stick around much is because I normally go to the games alone. Most importantly, I want to be safe, and it's best to leave before I enjoy myself and the cognac in my flask too much.

In November of 2016, my family headed to Orlando for a Thanksgiving retreat with Athena's relatives, and we rented a couple of houses that accommodated 10 to 15 people. The visit coincided with the Florida Classic on November 19, which pits Bethune-Cookman University against Florida A&M. I had no plans to attend the game, but on my birthday, November 17, my sister-in-law gifted me tickets to the Florida classic and a Polo shirt. Even my family understands and supports my love for HBCUs.

The game was played at Camping World Stadium in Orlando, Florida, which is an outstanding venue. The ultra-modern facility includes multiple giant video displays, two 360-degree concourses, a 20,000 square feet plaza deck, and indoor/outdoor club spaces that accommodate 5000 patrons. It has a 65,000-seat capacity, but no matter where you are in the stadium, you get an excellent view of the action on the field. The tailgate area had a decent crowd—not Magic City caliber—but plenty to mark this event as a must-attend. I did not try to coordinate or link up with any alums. I just wanted to go and take it all in, then head back to our accommodations. My brother-in-law and nephew accompanied me to the game. You could feel the excitement in the air. I wasn't inside the stadium 30 minutes before I saw a Hampton University alum rocking a Pirate shirt. Yes, he was violating Carlos' Classics etiquette, but there is nothing like seeing a familiar face in unfamiliar territory. We took a picture to send to other alums displaying Hampton pride in Orlando. Though I did not stay long, I enjoyed my time at the Florida Classic very much.

That year was my personal record for the number of classics I attended so far. However, since I am now retired, I have the time to better my 2016 effort. I have heard a lot of good things about the Aggie-Eagle Classic, which features North Carolina A&T against North Carolina Central University, and I have been plotting how to make my way to the Tar Heel state. I did not have any skin in the game between these two teams for a long time. But then, a cousin on my mom's side of the family enrolled at NCCU in the fall of 2019. He joined the Eagle football team, although he did not play much the first year, but he was moving up the depth chart. So, I had an incentive to put the classic on my schedule. Unfortunately, my cousin was killed on March 2, 2020 in Durham, North Carolina, apparently, in a tragic case of jealousy. The secondhand story I heard was that another member of the football team resented my cousin's efforts to move up depth chart and shot him. Now, it is even more important for me to make it to this game—in my cousin's honor.

There is one more classic I need to mention. It's the Southern Heritage Classic, which pits Jackson State against Tennessee State. The game takes place in Memphis, Tennessee and has been played annually since 1990, featuring the same two teams. It's a popular event. I was planning to go this year—my dad lives in Cordova, just outside of Memphis, and I was hoping to kill two birds with one stone—but the pandemic derailed my plans. Still, I figured if I didn't include it, I would not be able to go back to Jackson and show my face there.

I have highlighted several BCF classics, notably my favorites, but there are many more that anyone with a passion for the game can explore.

Chapter 7

FINANCES

Show me the money.
— Tom Cruise
in *Jerry Maguire*

Can there be too many classics? If every game becomes a classic, then none of them are. I understand the intent to market the game to places where there are a significant number of Black folks, but it adversely impacts a team's home game attendance. The home games are more important, as they affect a university's ability to generate funds to upgrade facilities. The average alums are going to review the football schedule and circle homecoming as the primary game to attend for the season. But if there is a classic scheduled, too, they will probably let it take precedence over a regular home game.

As a result, the classics attendance looks good—and the split of the take for the schools is 50/50—but turnout at home games, not so much. Even if a school has a good team, attendance and ticket sales may be down for the year, which will eat into the university's budget. Thus, schools have started requiring and charging for a ticket just to be in the tailgate area for the game, which rankles fans but makes financial sense. Some colleges are even leveraging their athletes to sell programs at the games, what I used to do at Mississippi Veterans Memorial Stadium. That cuts out opportunities for locals to contribute and make a little money, but they should not be ignored. But allowing the local population to assist in such efforts to enhance the games is important. That could lead to future enrollment of students and athletes for the schools, and, most importantly, lay the groundwork for future donors. I am not going to pretend that I understand the financial decisions that athletic departments make to balance the budget—that is for another time—but HBCUs should play fair with one another when monetary resources are limited.

Instead, a trend has emerged of schools fighting over the purse strings. In 2012, Alcorn exercised its rights to move the game against Jackson State back to its home in Lorman, Mississippi. Alcorn's leadership claimed that the city of Jackson did not provide enough compensation for its team to continue to play there. What I do know is: Lorman is not Jackson, and it does not have the capacity to host a historical rivalry game of such magnitude. The Jackson State versus Alcorn game divides families, pits high school teammates against each other, confirms bragging rights, and drives future recruiting efforts. None of that can take place in a small, minor venue.

I wonder if Alcorn is getting the payout it desired. It is true that every time the game is played in Lorman, Alcorn keeps most of the proceeds, but when it takes place in Jackson, Jackson State gets most of the money. You see, I have an undergraduate degree in finance. Although I have not put it to use in the military or civilian world, I understand the principles of time, value of money, and compound interest. I prefer to have the same payout annually rather than a seesaw every other year. Maybe there is more to it than I know, but I think the venue is the most important aspect of a classic game. I wonder if Alcorn is any better off since the game became a home and home series.

When HBCUs fight each other over limited resources, in the long run the football fans suffer, too. The folks that consistently buy tickets, travel to away games, and donate to the schools. The city of Jackson may not be what it used to be, but it still provides the best venue for the game. However, HBCUs must focus on what's best for Black College Football—not just what's in the best interest of Alcorn or Jackson State. Referring to the game as the Capital City Classic if it alternates between Jackson and Lorman is a misnomer and diminishes the event.

In 2013, the Whitewater Classic was established in Phenix City, Alabama, at Garrett-Harrison Stadium. The inaugural game pitted Tuskegee against Albany State. Phenix City's leadership wanted to attract more tourism to the city, and hosting a classic makes good business sense. Phenix City is only a stone's throw from Columbus with the Chattahoochee River serving as the physical border between the two cities. But, despite the games' proximity, I did not go. Many venues in this part of the south are just not very accommodating for large crowds. Like Garrett-Harrison, a lot of them are high school stadiums, which don't have the facilities to make attending the games enjoyable.

Alabama State's on-campus stadium offers a rather good venue to host a classic because it can accommodate a large crowd, and Montgomery is a convenient drive, but the decision to hold the game there goes back to financial resources. How much does it cost to play at the venue and how will proceeds be dispersed? Anywhere, cost can be minimized to maximize profits. The purpose of the game is to promote the Southern Intercollegiate Athletic Conference's football—both teams are SIAC members—but as a Division II event it doesn't feature many notable players for spectators to watch. Of course, who am I to say? It seems that the classic has met or exceeded expectations because there have been five games so far. And when its main competitor, the Tiger Classic, leaves nearby Columbus, the Whitewater Classic will continue to thrive.

In March 2020, Birmingham accepted the contract to host the Tiger Classic (Tuskegee University vs. Morehouse College). Being a larger city, Birmingham has more to offer than Columbus. In addition, Legion Field is a bigger venue. For me, the change—in a word—sucks! It did not take much for me to head to downtown Columbus for the game. Now, it would be a haul. Even though I am a TU sidewalk alum, I don't see myself traveling to Birmingham for this game. I'm not sure what the alum population for each school is in Birmingham, but I can't imagine a three-hour drive would entice a lot of members of the Morehouse community in Atlanta to go (compared to an hour and half to Columbus). Besides my own interest, I am looking at this game through the Magic City lens. There are notable alumnae and great fans on both sides, but I don't see them filling Legion Field. Both schools have small populations, which means smaller bands, diminishing the impact of their half-time shows. Still, I wish both schools well, and I hope they get the payouts they're looking for to invest in their schools and athletic programs.

As for the city of Columbus, I am still mad that it did not do more to keep the Tiger Classic, which it had hosted since 1935! Local officials have invested a significant amount of money to enhance its downtown, but they have not done anything to improve A.J. McClung Memorial Stadium. There are now more hotels and restaurants in downtown Columbus than one can shake a stick at. The city demolished the Booker T. Washington houses directly across the street from A.J. McClung Memorial Stadium and replaced them with new homes. There also are several softball fields that were used to support the Olympic Games when Atlanta hosted them in 1996. The Columbus Civic Center is by the stadium as well. But Columbus surely could have done more. I'm not certain Columbus even put up a fight to retain the classic. Perhaps the city officials felt that without it, they had one less headache to contend with.

Most people don't know that Columbus is the second largest city in Georgia. It can be misleading because Columbus is such a transient place, in part because of Fort Benning. There are people that live in Phenix City who have jobs in Columbus, as well as folks that commute from south Atlanta to work on the base. But as a city with a majority Black population, Columbus should never have lost this game.

I understand the impulse for the move to a larger venue because A.J. McClung Memorial Stadium only seats 15,000 people, but the city could have leveraged Fort Benning's presence to enhance the classic with displays and exhibits of Army equipment. The National Infantry Museum is one of the best military museums in the United States, and it's free. It has a monument dedicated to the 24th and 25th Black Infantry Regiments. Heck, the city could have requested a Blackhawk flyover to begin the game to appeal to the sizable number of veterans in the community. I may be reaching at this point, but if Columbus would not put measures in place to retain the Tiger Classic, it sent a clear message to other HBCUs that their games are not wanted there.

As much as I hate the creation of new classics, I realize that it is important to showcase Black College Football where it is welcomed and desired. Time will tell, and the supporters will speak. Let's face it, ultimately, we black fans are all we got when it comes to maintaining these classics. Instead of creating new classics, my money would be on bolstering support for the existing ones.

As I wrote this chapter in June 2020, I received two pieces of news that bothered me a lot.

I learned that the Orange Blossom Classic will pit Florida A&M University against Albany State at the Hard Rock Café Stadium in Miami on September 6, 2020. Per history, this classic was established in 1933. The first game featured FAMU and Howard University, and that rivalry continued for the next 45 years. The website for the classic does not provide a reason for the discontinuance of that rivalry. However, I surmise that lack of support, school participation, and an inadequate venue were contributing factors. So, nearly 45 years later, the game is being revived.

This is another example of what I don't like about just about every game being turned into a classic. I appreciate nostalgia as much as the next person, but not every game needs the classic moniker. It could just as well be an MEAC versus an SIAC team in a Labor Day kickoff game. Chicago Classic, Circle City Classic, and New York Urban League Classic are BCF's true classic games because they have endured through the years. Other classics that have been created should be discontinued to save resources. The in-state classics should continue to maintain their namesakes. But I wouldn't be surprised if the pursuit of increased bottom lines for HBCUs will carry the day.

The other news I received was that Florida A&M University's and Bethune-Cookman University's leadership plan to leave the Mid-Eastern Athletic Conference for the Southwestern Athletic Conference. I presume that this has to do with cost-saving measures. On Facebook, there was a lot of excitement over the possibility of FAMU joining the SWAC. Rattler nation is strong, and the move seems like a family reunion, almost as if FAMU should have been in the SWAC all along. FAMU's football team has not been competitive in the past 10 years or so. From 2011 to 2019, the Rattlers posted a 40-61 record. But in 2019, they had a 9-2 record, which looks like a return to dominance. Still, going to the SWAC would be a lateral move rather than an attempt at upward mobility, so what's the point? Of course, for FAMU's Marching 100, it makes all the sense in the world because the best bands are in the SWAC.

Other than fan excitement, I don't see how the SWAC leadership can perceive this poaching of another Black conference's team as a good move. In 2003, FAMU applied and was approved to move up to Division I-A, but it could not find a conference that would take it and played an independent schedule. A year later, it returned to I-AA status and joined the MEAC conference.

FAMU has the distinction of being the only HBCU to win a NCAA football championship. If the move happens, the university will have played in three of the four Black conferences, but to what end? Instead of letting FAMU jump conferences, the MEAC leadership could have adjusted the school's schedule to reduce travel costs and provide other incentives. If BCF is going to thrive, the leadership must get creative and make concessions, especially for a team like FAMU. After all, the Rattlers are one of the most recognizable brands in HBCUs, but, short of appropriate inducements to stay, I will admit that regionally this move makes sense for the Rattler Nation.

Chapter 8

IT HAPPENED ONLY ONCE

A champion is one who is remembered.
A legend is one who is never forgotten.

—Matshona Dhliwayo
philosopher, entrepreneur

In 1978, the Florida A&M Rattlers football team played the University of Massachusetts Minutemen in the Pioneer Bowl, an NCAA Division I-AA championship game. It was the first season of the I-AA football tournament, and the playoff bracket consisted of four teams. FAMU faced Jackson State in its semifinal game, and UMass challenged Villanova University. The draw worked out well because it insured that at least one HBCU team would compete in the championship game. At the time, FAMU was a member of the Southern Intercollegiate Athletic Conference (SIAC), which was an NCAA Division II conference, but it had been approved to join I-AA at the start of the 1978 season. The Pioneer Bowl took place on December 16 at Memorial Stadium in Wichita Falls, Texas, and FAMU defeated UMass 35-28 to become the only HBCU to ever win an NCAA Division I-AA championship, a unique and wonderful achievement.

The 1978 Rattlers went 12-1, with their only loss to Tennessee State University. Of note, the team's place kicker, Vince Coleman, went on to become a major league baseball player for the St. Louis Cardinals and was inducted into the team's Hall of Fame in 2018. The FAMU team he played on posted a 5-0 record in SIAC and captured that conference's championship crown as well. According to the Rattlers' school newspaper, the *FAMUAN*, "It's one of the greatest team that the school has ever fielded, and its legacy will endure."

I concur. The 1978 Rattlers hold the distinction of being the best HBCU football team in history, certainly until another HBCU wins an NCAA Division I football championship. Currently, such a victory would be a monumental accomplishment.

In 2013, the FCS expanded its tournament to 24 teams. At that time, Tennessee State was the only HBCU eligible to participate in the playoffs, essentially a four-percent chance to win—not the best odds for a HBCU to breakthrough. Once again, FAMU holds the distinction of being the last HBCU to win a playoff game. In 1999, the Rattlers defeated both Appalachian State (44-29) and Troy State (17-10), in road games, no less.

The Southwestern Athletic Conference (SWAC) gave up its automatic bid to the NCAA playoffs in 1999. This was a watershed moment in Black College Football and sent a terrible message: that Black colleges could not compete with the PWI schools in the NCAA despite their important legacy. The SWAC administrators surrendered the seat at the NCAA playoff table without putting up a fight. Had they been around when the SWAC received its automatic bid, I don't believe they would have let it go so easily.

Now, the conference can only boast a SWAC champion. I understand that money issues are different now, including travel costs to away games, but SWAC schools will schedule a "David versus

Goliath" contest for the potential of at least a $250,000 payout. But they don't want to compete with PWIs for a chance to be a NCAA football champion. It does not pass the logic test.

In the future, SWAC football players will have no shot at the NCAA title. The best that they can achieve is a SWAC championship. Subconsciously, it diminishes their incentive to sacrifice or try to be great because there is a glass ceiling on their efforts. A self-imposed glass ceiling.

As I think about how the SWAC gave up on the NCAA playoffs, I feel saddened and disgusted. Our ancestors endured almost 300 years of slavery, followed by another 100-year fight for Civil Rights. After 21 years of first-round losses, the SWAC leadership acted like little kids in a playground who, having lost a fight, take their marbles to play elsewhere and decided to not compete for the title. But SWAC basketball teams have not been competitive at the NCAA tournament either, yet the conference did not give up its automatic basketball bid.

I feel that the SWAC leadership took the easy way out. It had an equal opportunity as the other schools to compete for a national championship. Unfortunately, the conference's administrators are content with being the best Black football team only. This distinction is a de facto status because the CIAA and SIAC, the other two Black conferences, do not get a shot at the title.

Where does being the best Black anything advance the conferences' efforts to enhance, promote, and gain respect for the HBCU athletes? This type of mindset takes us right back to the back of the bus. As a career Army officer, I wished somebody would have said that I was a good Black officer, or that I was the finest officer from a HBCU, in recognition of my heritage and ability to succeed in the world at large.

The current conference leaders are perpetuating the myth that Blacks are subpar. I believe Black College Football players deserve better. We have fielded enough great athletes in the past to establish that the SWAC can develop elite players. We deserve a seat at the table!

Chapter 9

WHAT IS TO BE DONE?

Leaders must keep up with the times, educate themselves, be ready to innovate and care for their subordinates enough to think through how to succeed when old methods are clearly failing.

—Unknown

Restoring Black College Football to its former glory may be a tall order, but there are several things we can do. Here are some concrete proposals. Some may seem like wishful, pie-in-the-sky notions, but whoever said we shouldn't aim high?

My first suggestions is to replicate the NCAA college football playoffs and hold a Black National Championship competition. Since the SWAC and MEAC leaders have given away their seat at the NCAA playoff table, let's build a new one and seat the conferences we want to participate.

There already is a pseudo Black National Championship game, the Air Force Reserve Celebration Bowl created in 2015 and played annually in Atlanta. It features the MEAC and SWAC champions, which dismisses the importance of the CIAA and SIAC, the two oldest Black conferences. I know they are Division II, but how can the SWAC and MEAC declare a Black Football Champion and not include them? The CIAA and the SIAC should get a chance to compete and be crowned the Black College football champion. I don't think it's fair that they don't have the opportunity to participate.

It would work like this: I would not rig the system to guarantee that the MEAC and SWAC are pitted against each other in the final game. The seeding would be based on each team's overall record. For the semifinal games, the team with the better records would host the games at their home fields. Each conference would schedule its conference championship games earlier, and the semifinal games would take the slot they occupy now. This would allow the season to end without having to play any additional games, except for the championship contest. Also, the championship game would keep the Celebration Bowl's current slot to remain aligned with the NCAA bowl season. (That way, it would be clear that, while holding a Black college championship game, we continue to recognize the NCAA as the governing body for athletics.)

The two potential cities for the championship game are Atlanta or Charlotte, which have a lot of Black folks that enjoy a good event on a national stage. I would not want the game held at the Mercedes Benz Dome where the Atlanta Falcons play because I don't believe there would be enough support to fill it. It's not SEC football. Instead, Georgia State University's field presents a viable location. Furthermore, the championship game would need to be nationally televised. Considering that ESPN airs high school football games at times, I don't see why it would not be interested. If not, the OWN or Aspire network could provide coverage for the games. As for Charlotte as a venue, the Charlotte Hornets NBA team, which is owned by Michael Jordan, plays there—just trying to follow the money.

Needless to say, this would be a big boost for Black College Football.

(I don't want to be paid for my idea, but I would appreciate full access and VIP seats at the championship game.)

Some critics suggest that HBCUs are playing inferior football. To the degree that there is some truth to the criticism, I believe that it has a lot to do with coaching. Good coaches always improve teams and know how to optimize the talent they have. If you don't have the personnel to run a spread offense, play to your ability and run a pro-style offense or do both. As former Secretary of Defense Donald Rumsfeld once said, "You go to war with the Army you got not the one you want."

If you have success as a coach, don't rest on your laurels. Are you improving every year? Go to coaching clinics for self-development and get some smart assistants. I don't know if this is happening already, but if not, here is another suggestion that should be easy to accomplish. The National Football League has a host of Black coaching assistants that cannot get head coaching jobs. I know HBCUs don't have the budget to match an NFL salary, but they could sponsor coaching clinics to assist with Black College Football coaches' development.

At most HBCUs, the athletic facilities are subpar, and I imagine the coaching salaries are not lucrative. When a coach at a Black college starts winning, somebody from a PWI is going to make an attractive financial offer that is hard to refuse. The days of coaches like Eddie Robinson spending their whole career at one institution are probably gone. I find it hard to believe that no other university ever attempted to woo Coach Robinson away from Grambling, so the fact that he remained faithful all those years is remarkable. Given the current state of affairs, it is important for BCF programs to build their bench. Good coaches will be poached, and then its "next person up." Previously dominant Black college teams have been struggling because they change coaches as much as some people change their drawers.

To deal with the situation, athletic directors must be attuned to up-and-coming talent among their coaches. Similarly, university administrators must avoid nepotism and promote from within to maintain program continuity.

Another aspect of good coaching is player improvement. I remember that Coach Eddie Robinson's mentality was to develop all his players, but his primary focus was on better quarterback play. James Harris and Doug Williams were the beneficiaries of his efforts. Both starred in the NFL at a time when most considered Black quarterbacks inferior, incapable to compete at that level.

Again, Black assistant NFL coaches could help by providing support for players preparation, teaching offensive and defensive concepts used in the professional game. Then, BCF athletes would be better prepared for tryouts and interviews because they would understand the lingo and what teams look for in their players. As much as coaching development would enhance the play on the field, increasing athletes' chances to play in the NFL would be a win as well.

Furthermore, former star athletes at HBCUs, regardless of their sport, should give input on hiring a new football coach by serving on advisory or search committees. Technology is readily available with information about anybody's background, but it is nothing like an athlete's eye to determine if someone is a good fit or not. Most professional athletes possess distinctive leadership qualities that they can apply and readily recognize in coaching prospects. They also have built relationships across the sports industry that could expand a school's network for events or fundraising efforts, and contribute to improving its athletic program. For example, Deion "Prime Time" Sanders was announced as Jackson State's new football coach in September of 2020. Coach Prime is an NFL Hall of Famer and played Major League Baseball as well. I presume that Jackson State's baseball coach would connect with Coach Prime for some baseball contacts or tips to improve practice sessions.

It's important to be creative because the good old days are not coming back. The storied histories of the conferences only fall on deaf ears. To build for the future, commissioners need limited terms, and there should be age restrictions in place. Some folks don't want to pass the baton to a younger generation. Some folks don't know when to pass the baton. Some folks don't know how. Regardless, when there is no proper exchange, the baton usually falls helplessly to the ground. Then, it's finger-pointing time. Term limits will ensure that younger folks are being groomed for increased responsibilities. That would inspire individuals to return to their alma maters to become leaders there. More importantly, they will come with fresh ideas and a willingness to try them out.

Another significant and underappreciated audience is women. Football is a traditionally male dominated sport, and females are relegated to medical support, dancing lines or band membership. But Black College Football is our game, and Black women deserve a larger stake in it. Black women are unique and possess qualities that are game changers regardless whether or not they are allowed to play the game. Black women are creative, broker deals, and serve with conviction in all their endeavors. As an army officer who happened to be black, I know what it's like to be marginalized and treated as if I had no voice. I witnessed firsthand how it happened even more to black women. When I worked with black female officers, I always tried to serve as a sounding board, providing information, and support their decisions so they knew I had their back.

I just finished an excellent book about Ella Baker, and it got me thinking. In *Ella Baker: Community Organizer of the Civil Rights Movement*, author J. Todd Moye showed that she was a stalwart in the struggle for Civil Rights. Ella Baker was so independent that she maintained her maiden name when she got married. She worked for both the NAACP and the Southern Christian Leadership Conference (SCLC). The consistent theme throughout the book was that she always championed the cause to secure American citizenship for African Americans.

Unfortunately, neither organization ever gave her a key leadership position or allowed her to speak truth to power. But Ella Baker was not daunted. She continued to organize and is considered to be the mother of the Student Non-Violent Coordinating Committee, better known as SNCC. Its young members were responsible for the lunch counter sit-ins, Freedom Rides, and community organizing in the South during the Civil Rights Movement. Ella Baker was an immensely powerful woman who does not always get her due.

As I read about her, it became clear to me that our culture cannot achieve prominence without deliberately and consistently including Black women in the work.

It's time for Black women to receive leadership opportunities and a voice in Black College Football. Some strides have been made as HBCUs boast a few female athletic directors, notably Dr. Ingrid Wicker McCree at North Carolina Central University and Dr. Kiki Baker Barnes at Dillard University, but much more can be done.

Throughout American history, it has been Black women leading the charge for citizenship and equal opportunities for Black folks. They organized behind the scenes and encouraged their menfolk to vote long before the 19th Amendment to the U.S. Constitution guaranteed their own right to go to the ballot box. Imagine what power they would bring to further Black College Football! BCF needs its Black women on the front lines and in leadership positions.

In that light, I would like to discuss sports journalist Jemele Hill's provocative proposal that Black athletes leave white colleges to attend HBCUs. She presented this idea to address the financial gap between predominantly white institutions and HBCUs athletics. Black athletes generate billions of dollars for PWIs that lead to new buildings to support academics and athletic programs. I think this would work well for basketball because there are fewer players on basketball rosters and travel costs are significantly lower. Basketball is not a full-contact sport so when HBCUs schedule to play bigger schools, the probability of catastrophic injuries during games is not a concern. The three-point line serves as the great equalizer, so taller teams are not guaranteed victories. Most importantly, the teams could compete for the NCAA championship.

Black leaders with a platform must call for the change they want to see. It is significant that, although Jemele Hill did not attend an HBCU, she would suggest that top athletes do so. But do not urge someone to do something that you are not willing to support with your human or financial capital. HBCUs are our 40 acres and a mule, so we need to be tilling our land to produce the future leaders.

I like this idea, but I don't believe it will happen anytime soon in football, because HBCUs don't have the infrastructure, technical support, medical staff, booster backing, or money to bolster their football programs. Most importantly, there is the lack of a quality medical staff.

Dr. James Andrews is an orthopedic surgeon and sports medicine specialist, affiliated with Auburn University, the University of Alabama, and the Tampa Bay Rays. He is usually on the sidelines during their games, and when there is an injury to a player, he either intervenes directly or supervises the treatment. Football players at AU and Alabama can return to the field in a matter of weeks. Imagine if Dr. Andrews were patrolling the sidelines at Alabama State or Alabama A&M. God only knows how much Bama and AU pay Dr. Andrews, but that's the type of capability that BCF needs. It's great to have five-star recruits, but if you cannot keep them healthy and receiving top-notch medical care, they will spend more time on the sidelines.

On September 26, 2015, when Southern University played the University of Georgia, Devon Gales, a SU football player, suffered a paralyzing spinal injury during a kickoff return. Football players can get hurt at any level of competition, but this game did not have to take place because there was no history or conference connection requiring these two teams to meet. (I credit Georgia's administration making every effort to support Gales' medical care.) I feel for Gale and his family because their lives have been significantly changed. It was good to hear of his return to football in 2019, four years after his injury and rehab, as an assistant coach for the Jefferson High School Dragons in Jefferson, Georgia.

Of course, there are bigger issues at play here as well. Follow me for a minute here: Southern University is in Baton Rouge, Louisiana. I could understand a game against LSU due to proximity which would be a lot of fun for Baton Rouge residents. But SU traveling to Athens, Georgia, to play an SEC school? The Bulldogs come close to being a pro team. So why have this game at all? Because of money. Everybody knew it when the contest was scheduled. Unfortunately, Gale suffered a significant injury. Just like in any other contact sport, the critics came out to question why HBCUs are playing these kinds of games. The extra money should improve the football team and other athletic programs, but by the time the university's bureaucratic laundromat washes it, there is rarely a direct correlation with the game. Also, after the bills are paid for travel, lodging, and food, there is not much left in the account. Still, I don't actually mind these games because I think it gives BCF coaches and players something to aspire to.

But if the money is not going directly to the football team or the athletic department, it defeats the whole purpose of scheduling these types of games. It appears that university administrators are pimping the football team to pay the light or the grocery bill, and the football team is not any better off the following year—no new weightlifting facilities, medical trainers, or strength coaches. If HBCUs are going to continue to play these games, the university should be held accountable and transparent. When I am watching a HBCU team get crushed, I should be able to reach out to an alum of that school to learn how the proceeds from the game are benefiting the athletic department.

Alums have the power to improve and enhance fiscally challenged teams. These efforts can lead to better facilities, cover travel expenses, pay for laundry, team meals, and even an additional medical staff member if enough is donated. Without the facilities, no four- or five-star recruit will entertain the notion of attending any HBCUs. Also, better facilities can change an average player to a good player, or a good player to a great player. The collection plate needs to be circulated among alums to assist with the upgrade of facilities. School spirit is one thing, but cheerful givers is what many HBCUs really need.

It is funny how regular folks are always trying to tell celebrities and star athletes what to do with their money. But Black luminaries need to donate to HBCUs. Voila, there it is! Financial gap closed. Again, another unlikely event, but we might as well shoot for the stars. I marveled at Odell Beckham Jr. and LeBron James donating Beats headphones to Louisiana State University and Ohio State University. In Beckham's case, it's his alma mater, but LeBron is Ohio's native son and an Ohio State football megafan. Maybe, LeBron has sent a couple of dollars to Wilberforce University or Central State University already. If not, they would be excellent candidates for benefiting from his generosity.

LeBron has done a lot, so I do not mean to single him out, but other Black star athletes should follow his lead. By the way, both of the above schools have superb alum and booster support.

Again, I know celebrities have busy schedules, but if they would buy a ticket to a game or even a fish plate if they happen to be in town when there is a classic or BCF game, it would be helpful. If they cannot make it to the game, they could add some HBCU apparel to their wardrobes and flex on Instagram. It would go a long way to promote BCF culture.

I know Bill Cosby, as a convicted sex offender serving prison time, is persona non grata, and his past achievements have been dismissed. However, I grew up watching *The Cosby Show* and *A Different World*, and Dr. Huxtable's in-show children sported HBCU apparel in several episodes. Spike Lee is another celebrity who often represents his HBCU alma mater, Morehouse College, in his movies. I just watched *Da 5 Bloods*, and one of the characters was wearing a Morehouse shirt. Black folks also displayed a great deal of pride for the Black Panther movie. Everybody was yelling, "Wakanda Forever!" The star of the movie, Chadwick Bozeman (whose recent death at such a young age due to cancer was saddening and reverberated throughout the Black community) was a Howard University alum. So, how about "Black College Football forever!"

When I traveled to Auburn University's campus for Army Reserve Officer's Training Corps meetings, I was always amazed by the student body's support for the school. I mean, every student was decked out in some type of Auburn gear with accessories—not just shirts, but shoes, socks, bikes, sunglasses. I did not notice anyone with an NFL jersey. It was like a total war concept. You were either an Auburn Tiger or an interloper. HBCUs could learn from this example. Students on campus should only sport their school's colors and not some other school's attire. I taught Army ROTC at Columbus State University in Georgia. CSU does not have a football team. I noticed students on my campus with Auburn, Alabama, Georgia and other schools' clothing, but not much CSU gear. I made it appoint to sport CSU apparel when I was not required to wear a military uniform. I was a proud CSU Cougar and I still wear the colors today.

In July 2019, LSU unveiled its $28 million football operation center. It is a state-of-the-art facility, including a nutritional program for all student athletes. Tyrann Mathieu, a former player, donated $1 million for its construction. During the 2016-2017 school year, Prairie View generated the highest HBCU donations for the entire athletic program at just under $18 million. This

further highlights the financial disparity between elite university football and BCF. This goes back to Auburn's "total war" approach. Former players and alums must be willing to give back
financially or with their human capital to their Black alma maters.
In addition, HBCUs need the support of the local communities
to fill stadiums on game days and support fundraising activities.
Until there are concerted efforts, the financial gap will continue
to widen. Ultimately, the overall product continues to diminish.
I know I am not the only one that feels this way. I am sure there
have been more ideas that I am not privy to.

HBCU leaders, it's time to do something! Here's an extreme
proposal: Either terminate football or eliminate some other, un-
popular sport so more money can be allocated to the football
program.

I love all HBCUs. I don't want to see any more closed. I don't
have an issue with defending their existence. I believe if they can
shut down one HBCU, they can shut down all of them. Some
HBCUs have big-time donors, law schools, medical schools, and
other top-notch programs, so there is no imminent threat to
them. However, those schools that depend on state funding and
are poorly run are constantly at risk. This correlates directly to
Black College Football.

King Christophe, a key leader during the Haitian Revolution
and president of Haiti said, "We lack pride, and we do not have
pride because we don't have memories." There needs to be an en-
hanced sense of pride for all HBCUs and less trolling. For example, when there is a negative news item about an HBCU, there
are usually comments on Twitter and Instagram by other Blacks,
like, "That wouldn't happen at our school." It's the opposite side
of the coin of revoking someone's Black card for not being Black

enough, and it's counterproductive at best. If we don't care about our game, no one else will. It will be like Eddie Robinson, Walter Payton, Jerry Rice, Willie Totten, Archie Coolie, Lewis Tillman, W. C. Gorden, Steve McNair, and many others never existed. For me, they are seared in my memory, and I swell with pride because I can keep their BCF exploits achievements alive.

CONCLUSION

To each there comes in their lifetime a special moment when they are figuratively tapped on the shoulder and offered the chance to do a very special thing, unique to them and fitted to their talents. What a tragedy if that moment finds them unprepared or unqualified for that which could have been their finest hour.

—Winston Churchill

Black College Football is not dead, but it's on a ventilator.

Should we let it slip into a coma and expire? If you've read this far, you know my opinion. Heck, no!

But the athletes, administrators, and alums are not enough for it to breathe freely on its own. Getting the best players and coaches would surely help, but schools also need to market the talent that they have. It starts with getting the local community behind it through ticket sales. The BCF games that I have supported in recent years have fallen short of my expectations. I am used to seeing at least 40,000 folks in the stadium. If it's not a classic or homecoming you will be lucky if there are 20,000 in the stands. However, tailgating is the new norm. I don't mind a good tailgate, but I prefer a competitive game with skilled players. I watched a BCF game on the Aspire Network in 2019. It seemed as though there was a turnover every other play—just poor execution all around. The bands were doing their thing, which is always entertaining, but I was more interested in who the marquee players were. It was impossible to tell. The game was disappointing to say the least.

Because of the COVID pandemic, Morehouse College canceled fall sports, including football, for the 2020 season. I was also disappointed when the Tiger Classic moved to Birmingham, but now there will not be a game at all. I'm pretty sure that many schools will follow suit. Other HBCUs have canceled homecoming activities as well, but not the games at the point I'm writing this.

The Southeastern Conference is the premier conference in the NCAA, so it will be interesting to see what its leadership decides to do about its season. These are uncertain times, and I have prepared myself for life with no football in 2020. However, your average fan may not fare well without football because it is life for a lot of people. I enjoy college football, but I am not a fanatic. So, it strikes me as funny how the sports world will go to great lengths to have a season despite everything happening in the world, spending money that could be put to better use. For example, the National Basketball Association made plans to play a shortened season because it has the resources to test everyone affiliated with the game. The NBA created a bubble at the Walt Disney World Resort, Orlando, Florida inside the ESPN Wide World of Sports Complex. There were only 22 teams allowed in. Each team could only have a roster of 37 people, which included coaches, players, trainers, strength coaches, equipment managers and security. Imagine if the money to pay for all that had been repurposed and donated to help kids return safely to school?

Since COVID-19, I have changed and adapted. I'm retired from the Army and fortunate that my pension and disability payment sustain me through this crisis. As such, I don't leave the house unless it's absolutely necessary because I feel I am doing my part to look out for my fellow citizens. I don't believe I will be attending any games this year. In the meantime, we can take stock and, hopefully, have a real discussion about the future of Black College Football. This book is a call to start a conversation in the Black community to do more. I challenge you to wear some paraphernalia, attend sporting events safely, or simply donate to a HBCU annually.

During the time I was writing this book, George Floyd was murdered by members of the Minneapolis police. This event sparked protests across the country with the Black Lives Matter movement at the forefront. While I wouldn't expect that kind of mobilization to ensure that BCF endures for years to come, such passionate support for the cause would go a long way toward making it happen.

HBCUs were established to educate Black folks after slavery. Yet, after assimilation and access to attend the university of their choice, Black folks are split about the importance of maintaining HBCUs. There has been a lot of discussion through the years about reparations for African Americans, but we will not invest in our own institutions which were created for our advancement.

I know some people struggle with the notion of supporting Black businesses just because they are Black. However, it's a challenge that they should take on. I understand that it is asking a lot and doesn't always pass the logic test. However, most Black folks that I know only allow Black barbers or hairdressers to do their hair.

The other side of this coin is Black folks' attitude about money. Like Cedric the Entertainer exclaimed, "I ain't got it all, but I can put something on it." It's the mismanagement of funds that lands some HBCUs in trouble and brings them to the brink of closure. The headlines about how some HBCU president has misappropriated funds tarnish the reputation of those schools. That is not to say that such activities don't occur at PWIs, too, but the impact is incredibly damaging for HBCUs and not easily remedied. Still, while we all have had bad experiences with Black businesses regarding customer service and high prices, and disappointment with unscrupulous HBCU leaders, that is no reason for us to turn our backs on them. Yes, there will be ups and down supporting businesses and organizations that cater to Black people, but it is worth it.

Black folks cringe at being called out in public, especially if their alma mater made the hit list. Kinfolk, that statement is not meant as a sucker punch, but rather a call to arms. It's about personal accountability to do more to spread the word, donate money, and/or contribute a service to promote BCF.

"The main hope of a nation lies in the proper education of its youth." I wasn't sure where I got this quote from, so I looked it up. It was by Erasmus, a Dutch philosopher during the Renaissance. He was right then, and he is right now. Education is a key to opportunities. In our community, there are schools in place for our young people, and we must support them.

As I was writing this book, many people asked me why I thought it is important. The only real answer I had is that I have some positive energy to put in the atmosphere about something I care deeply about: Black College Football. I get calls about a lot of things, but, surprisingly, most of them are about the state of HBCUs. As a committed supporter of those schools and, especially, Black College Football, it is a part of my DNA. More importantly, I lived it, love it, and want to keep living and loving it. I hope to do a retrospective 20 years from now when a new generation takes our game to new heights. It is my hope that my effort creates ripples that will reach the football players and athletic departments at HBCUs, their alums, the fans of the games, and the people in the cities and towns where Black College Football classics take place. I want them to appreciate the history of our game and know its key figures so that they are not lost in time. Or in my case, tucked away in precious memories. I am always ready and willing to share my experiences with anyone who will listen. With this book, I hope I am received as a griot that begets another and another…

ACKNOWLEDGMENTS

When I started this endeavor, I told my wife, and she scoffed, "How you going to write a second book and you ain't finished the first one?" I had been working on a book about taking care of my mom, but when the ideas for this book took over, I set it aside. Athena's reaction did not surprise me. That is her temperament and her response to my many crazy ideas. It's not to demean me but to give me a dose of reality.

On the flip side, if this book takes off and I get requests for interviews, you already know who's going to pull up right next to me: my wife. No way she would allow me to bask in the spotlight alone. And that is just fine. After all, Athena has supported me by giving me the space to share my story, and I thank her for it with all my heart.

To my wife, I love you and thank you for all that you do.

To my daughters, Chassidy and Camille. I just want you to dream the impossible and get to work. Dream no small dreams for they are yours to be as big as your endeavors.

I thank God for life.

To my parents for settling in Jackson, Mississippi. Thanks to my mom for my love of music, the black coach and the black quarterback. To my dad for my work ethic and self-discipline.

Salute to K. Rich for the conversation that provided the spark to get me started on the book.

Thanks to Tucker Max and Zach Obront for *The Scribe Method*, my guide and excellent reference in this undertaking.

Thanks to Cathleen Shaw of the Shaw Consulting Group for the book cover design and linking me up with Chris Angermann.

To Chris, from our first conversation, we were kindred spirits. Thanks for challenging me and believing in my manuscript. I appreciate the quiet whispers to prepare me for my pilgrimage to Mecca.

There were friends and family members that I shared chapters with, who I also thank. They know who they are. Everybody gave me exactly what I needed; not necessarily what I wanted. Thank all of you for taking the time to support me.

Appendix — HBCUs

Not every Historical Black College or University has football teams. But all of them continue to fulfill a mission of making higher education accessible to African Americans. Below is a list of all HBCUs.

Alabama A & M University	4-year, Public
Alabama State University	4-year, Public
Albany State University	4-year, Public
Alcorn State University	4-year, Public
Allen University	4-year, Private
Arkansas Baptist College	4-year, Private
Benedict College	4-year, Private
Bennett College	4-year, Private
Bethune-Cookman University	4-year, Private
Bishop State Community College	2-year, Public
Bluefield State College	4-year, Public
Bowie State University	4-year, Public
Central State University	4-year, Public
Cheyney University of Pennsylvania	4-year, Public
Claflin University	4-year, Private
Clark Atlanta University	4-year, Private
Clinton College	4-year, Private
Coahoma Community College	2-year, Public
Coppin State University	4-year, Public
Delaware State University	4-year, Public
Denmark Technical College	2-year, Public
Dillard University	4-year, Private

Edward Waters College	4-year, Private
Elizabeth City State University	4-year, Public
Fayetteville State University	4-year, Public
Fisk University	4-year, Private
Florida Agricultural and Mechanical University	4-year, Public
Florida Memorial University	4-year, Private
Fort Valley State University	4-year, Public
Gadsden State Community College	2-year, Public
Grambling State University	4-year, Public
H. Councill Trenholm State Community College	2-year, Public
Hampton University	4-year, Private
Harris-Stowe State University	4-year, Public
Hinds Community College-Utica	2-year, Public
Howard University	4-year, Private
Huston-Tillotson University	4-year, Private
Interdenominational Theological Center	4-year, Private
Jackson State University	4-year, Public
Jarvis Christian College	4-year, Private
Johnson C. Smith University	4-year, Private
Kentucky State University	4-year, Public
Lane College	4-year, Private
Langston University	4-year, Public
Lawson State Community College	2-year, Public
LeMoyne-Owen College	4-year, Private
Lincoln University	4-year, Public
Livingstone College	4-year, Private
Meharry Medical College	4-year, Private
Miles College	4-year, Private
Mississippi Valley State University	4-year, Public
Morehouse College	4-year, Private

Morehouse School of Medicine	4-year, Private
Morgan State University	4-year, Public
Morris College	4-year, Private
Norfolk State University	4-year, Public
North Carolina A & T State University	4-year, Public
North Carolina Central University	4-year, Public
Oakwood University	4-year, Private
Paine College	4-year, Private
Paul Quinn College	4-year, Private
Philander Smith College	4-year, Private
Prairie View A & M University	4-year, Public
Rust College	4-year, Private
Saint Augustine's University	4-year, Private
Savannah State University	4-year, Public
Selma University	4-year, Private
Shaw University	4-year, Private
Shelton State Community College – C. A. Freed Campus	2-year, Public
South Carolina State University	4-year, Public
Southern University and A & M College	4-year, Public
Southern University at New Orleans	4-year, Public
Southern University at Shreveport	2-year, Public
Southwestern Christian College	4-year, Private
Spelman College	4-year, Private
Stillman College	4-year, Private
Talladega College	4-year, Private
Tennessee State University	4-year, Public
Texas College	4-year, Private
Texas Southern University	4-year, Public
Tougaloo College	4-year, Private

Tuskegee University	4-year, Private
University of Arkansas at Pine Bluff	4-year, Public
University of Maryland Eastern Shore	4-year, Public
University of the District of Columbia	4-year, Public
University of the Virgin Islands	4-year, Public
Virginia State University	4-year, Public
Virginia Union University	4-year, Private
Virginia University of Lynchburg	4-year, Private
Voorhees College	4-year, Private
West Virginia State University	4-year, Public
Wilberforce University	4-year, Private
Wiley College	4-year, Private
Winston-Salem State University	4-year, Public
Xavier University of Louisiana	4-year, Private

Index

A

Aeneas Williams 12
Aggie-Eagle Classic 63
A. J. McClung Memorial Stadium 61
Archie Coolie 88

B

Barack Obama, President 60
Bayou Classic 12, 56
Birmingham, Alabama 8, 11, 12, 13, 56, 57, 61, 68, 92, 101

C

Callaway High School 17, 18, 19
Camping World Stadium 63
Capital City Classic 52, 67
Chadwick Boseman 87
Chicago Classic 56, 70
Circle City Classic 56, 70
Columbus, Georgia 11, 14, 56, 61, 62, 67, 68, 69, 87
Columbus State 87

D

Dancing Dolls 37
Darion Connor 19, 25
Deondre Francois 43
Devon Gales 84
Don Cheadle 12
Doug Williams 33, 34, 35, 80

E

Eddie Robinson, Coach 12, 29, 31, 33, 34, 36, 37, 60, 79, 80, 88
Ella Baker 82

F

Florida A&M University 9, 11, 59, 63, 70, 75
Florida Classic 11, 13, 62, 63
Fountain City Classic 58, 62

G

Grambling State University 8, 12, 13, 24, 27, 29, 30, 31, 32, 33, 34, 35, 36, 37, 52, 55, 56, 79, 101
Grambling Tigers 12, 15, 19, 25, 26, 27, 31, 34

H

Hampton University 11, 25, 31, 39, 40, 41, 42, 43, 44, 45, 56, 57, 58, 61, 63, 101
Hampton University Pirates 39, 40, 42, 44, 45
Human Jukebox Marching Band 33

I

Ingrid Wicker McCree, Dr. 82
Isaac Holt 50
Isaiah Crowell 43

J

Jackie Robinson 60
Jackson State Blue Bengals 15, 20, 25, 26, 30, 31, 36, 49, 51, 53
Jackson State University 8, 15, 17, 18, 19, 20, 21, 22, 24, 25, 26, 27, 30, 31, 35, 36, 37, 41, 45, 47, 48, 49, 50, 51, 52, 64, 66, 67, 73, 81, 101

Jake Reed 12
James Harris 80
Jemele Hill 20, 83
Jay "Sky" Walker 47,54
Jerry Rice 19, 49, 50, 51, 53, 88
Jim Gregory 37
Joe Taylor, Coach 39
John Thompson, Coach 34
Junious "Buck" Buchanan 29

K

Kiki Baker Barnes, Dr. 82
K. Rich 11, 12, 13, 56, 57, 58, 62, 97

L

Ladd-Pebbles Stadium 59
Legion Field 12, 57, 68
Lewis Tillman 19, 25, 88

M

Magic City Classic 11, 12, 56, 58, 61, 62, 63, 68
Marching 100 71
Marching Storm 33
Melvin Spears, Coach 34
Michelle Obama 27
Mississippi Veterans Memorial Stadium 19, 22, 27, 65

N

Negro League 60
New York Urban League Classic 56, 70

O

Orange Blossom Classic 70

P

Pioneer Bowl 73
Powell Junior High School 16, 17

R

Robert Johnson 14

S

Shannon Boyd 19
Sonic Boom of the South Marching Bank 22, 23, 30, 31, 33
Southern Heritage Classic 45, 64
Steve McNair 19, 47, 51, 53, 89

T

Tiger Classic 58, 61, 62, 68, 69, 92

V

Vince Coleman 73

W

Walter Payton 19, 88
W. C. Gorden, Coach 30, 89
Whitewater Classic 67
Willie Totten 49, 88

Carlos A. Lock is a native of Jackson, Mississippi. He grew up a Jackson State fan and lived Southwestern Athletic Conference football for a decade —football is in his DNA. He attended Hampton University, a Mid-Eastern Athletic Conference school, and graduated with a Bachelor of Science in Finance. He also has a Master of Arts in Higher Education from the University of Louisville.

A retired U.S. Army Lieutenant Colonel, Carlos served two combat tours to Afghanistan and Iraq. As a certified logistics professional, he has earned several awards, most notably the Bronze Star.

Carlos lives with his wife, mother and two daughters in Columbus, Georgia, and attends as many BCF games and classics as he can.